14 GREAT GAMES
OLDHAM ATHLETIC

To Andy
Best wishes
2015

14 GREAT GAMES
OLDHAM ATHLETIC

RICK HOLDEN & DAVE MOORE

14 GREAT GAMES
OLDHAM ATHLETIC

© Rick Holden & Dave Moore

Rick Holden and Dave Moore have asserted their rights in accordance with the Copyright, Designs & and Patents Act 1988 to be identified to be the authors of this work.

Published by:

Wi/\le Publishing

British Columbia, Canada
Email: info@wibblepublishing.com
Web: www.wibblepublishing.com

First published 2015

Legal Deposit: Library and Archives Canada, Ottawa, Ontario, Canada.

13-digit ISBN: 978-1-987860-00-9

Printed in Great Britain

FOREWORD

It seems an appropriate time to reflect on some of the finest moments in Oldham Athletic's history as it is over twenty years since we achieved what most fans thought would be unachievable in modern football – the 'Holy Grail' of Latics in the top flight! This book gives a unique and most eloquent insight into not only the matches and how they were played out, but also the inside view of how the players saw the games and the feel of what was happening inside the club. It came at a time that was the peak of not only the club's achievements but also, arguably, the best times that the players involved ever had in professional football. Although some went on to greater things, I doubt they experienced the togetherness and camaraderie that we had at the time.

The game against my former club, Ipswich Town, and the Championship winning game against Sheffield Wednesday were the highlights of my career. I am immensely proud to have played my part in what was undoubtedly the best period in Oldham Athletic's long history and probably always will be. There can be no-one better than Rick to provide this insight as he played in all of the games; he also tells it exactly 'how it was' at the time in his own inimitable style! - *Jon Hallworth (Former goalkeeper of Ipswich Town, Oldham Athletic, Cardiff City, Newport County and Bangor City)*

INTRODUCTION – RICK

It has only just dawned on me in the last year or so as to how lucky I was to be involved in such a unique time, some twenty odd years ago, when we, at Oldham, finally won a trophy. We had of course started our rise two years earlier than our triumph on that most amazing of days at home in May 1991 in the match against Sheffield Wednesday.

This book charters fourteen important games that I was involved in, in that magical era, and is written to give you an insight into the atmosphere at the time in and around the team and the town. I have written the inside story on the team and its management from within as a player and Dave Moore has written it from the outside as a fan following the team and yet very much part of that all important twelfth man. Our superb Latics' fans, who followed us everywhere, were finally rewarded with that one famous game which saw us win a trophy. There is tragedy and ultimate triumph for arguably the best team in the history of Oldham Athletic which saw them bring great sides to their knees as well as putting their fans through hell and back.

The story goes beyond into the top flight to show the outpouring of emotion once we had reached the promised land; we entertained Chelsea at home for the first game of the 1991/2 season and fought the amazing battle against Notts County which secured survival in the top flight in the same year, but mainly it concentrates on the growing of this team from 1989 until 1994 and the key games that got us there!

These, I am sure you will agree as avid fanatics of your favourite team, are 'never to be forgotten games' and I hope you enjoy reading our side of the events as much as I did playing in these amazing games.

This was Joe Royle's team which he built out of almost nothing and the likes of which will probably not be realised again anywhere in England. Every player at Oldham at the time went on to become a household name and had excellent careers which will probably not happen again either! Joe Royle was chasing a dream of getting Oldham into the old First Division which was preposterous when you look back at it now from 2014 but he had his vision and his methods, and he selected his players who ultimately carried it off which was an outstanding feat when you reflect on the achievements.

I hope that this book inspires players and fans to repeat what we did and I sincerely hope they can, and the recent Oldham win in the FA Cup over Liverpool certainly brought a tear to my eye and proves that, with belief and hard work, anything is possible.

Rick Holden 2015

INTRODUCTION – DAVE

I consider myself very fortunate to have followed my team, Oldham Athletic, since the 1959/60 season and in that time I have witnessed more ups and downs than you could encounter in a lifetime of playing perpetual snakes and ladders. I have witnessed lows like re-election and relegation as well as the highs of promotion from the Fourth Division in the Bobby Johnston era. I have also encountered the rise to the Second Division under Jimmy Frizzell and more recently witnessed the 'pinch me' years which was achieved under the Latics' most successful manager of all time, Joe Royle.

It has been a roller coaster journey and, particularly in recent years, could be likened to having to serve a prison sentence for a crime you didn't commit. That about sums up what being a true fan of a club is. If you don't experience the bad times how can you appreciate the good times? It would be boring to support one of the 'so-called' big teams who were winning every week so I have no regrets with my experiences although it has brought tears and despondency at times.

When Rick mooted the idea of penning a record of what he considered to be his fourteen greatest games for Oldham Athletic, in what was arguably regarded as the best ever Latics era, I had no hesitation about being included in the venture. Rick wanted an anatomy of what it was like, both as a player and as a fan, so I had no doubts about giving my side of the story along with some musings and opinions from other Oldham Athletic supporters.

All fans will argue about which matches they consider to be the best and, when they have discussed it, many differing opinions always throw up a huge variety of *best* games which could be argued forever but there can be no arguing with the selection in this book as they were *ALL* great games.

I also consider it a slightly worrying task and I regard it to be a huge responsibility to portray my own opinions about the games as a representative of so many other people who could do an equally admirable job. The matches occurred in such an epoch of the existence of the club that it affected the whole town of Oldham and not just one individual. I therefore decided to seek out and obtain as many differing opinions as to what made this particular period such an exciting and unbelievable event in the history of Oldham Athletic AFC. I hope we have done it justice.

Dave Moore 2015

DEDICATION

To Joe Royle

ACKNOWLEDGEMENTS

The authors would like to acknowledge the following for their assistance is the writing of *'14 Great Games – Oldham Athletic.'* The *Oldham Evening Chronicle,* Jon Hallworth, Andy Ritchie, Kevin Anderson (Fryatt), Phil Stevenson, Barry Noble, Bob Fleming, Colin Heaton, Ollie Green, Mick Cunningham, Martin Bell, David Lloyd, Phil Taylor and a miriad of Oldham Athletic supporters who prefer to remain anonymous or have contributed by social media formats and through club message boards.

CONTENTS

The Philosophy of Football .... or the reasons behind the success

The most frequent questions that I am asked are, "What was the reason behind Oldham's success?" and "What was it like in the dressing room?" The following is an attempt to answer these two questions, but obviously it is just my take on it. Indeed this book is *my* account of the years of success and this is why it centres round *me*.

Most dressing rooms in football clubs at any level have one or two characters who are, shall we say, a little bit different. For whatever quirk they have in their make-up they usually add spice to the atmosphere in more often than not a positive way. Correspondingly, some personalities are disruptive and have a negative effect on the environment if they are allowed to get away with it. Who prevents the disruptive one or two from getting away with it and causing disharmony? The manager, most would say, must do this and perhaps the team captain. The answer is to have more than a few crazy positive characters within the group and they will sort it.

To give an example of this we signed Neil McDonald from Everton, and he brought an air of gloom and negativity with him. He appeared to be a dour character and I can remember instantly thinking that this bloke is going to struggle in here. His position in the changing room was sandwiched between Neil Redfearn and Mick Milligan, with Ian Marshall in dangerous proximity, although he didn't have to endure Redders for long. It wasn't that Macca was a bad character but we knew he was gloomy and didn't want to be at little Oldham. It didn't take long for him to start getting it; it also didn't help that he would arrive second last every day for training, just before Doddy (David Currie) who was always last, so the lads were all sitting there waiting for him to turn up.

If you wanted to keep a low profile at any club, and especially this one, arrive before anyone else. You are less likely to get ripped about the gear you are wearing and your general demeanour. So I quickly got stuck into Macca by singing the first line of AC/DC's *Hells Bells* track which goes, *'Roaring thunder pouring rain, I'm coming on like a hurricane'* every time he appeared to give the impression of doom and gloom. At first he didn't twig, but very soon he did when all the lads started singing it on his arrival, with the added effect of Marshy standing above him and simulating lightning strikes and rain with his fingers on top of his head while making realistic sound effects of a thunderstorm. He could have cracked and gone under but, to his credit, he began to take it and even started singing it to himself when he arrived. To this day if he ever sends a text or calls one of the lads – he is particularly good friends with Jon 'Captain' Hallworth – he addresses himself as, *'it's Roaring Thunderheed here.....'*

That gives you an insight into what our dressing room could be like. I would call it very positive crazy humour although the word 'crazy' conjures up another image in our football. Around at the same time, but slightly earlier, was Wimbledon Football Club which was quickly christened 'The Crazy Gang.' They had, of course, captured the nation's attention by a meteoric rise from non-league football to winning the FA Cup against Liverpool and maintaining top flight status for several seasons. This was much to the annoyance of many of football's self-proclaimed purists. What stuck in the craw about this lot was a combination of factors which all led to this synopsis of their overall behaviour. They were the paupers from Plough Lane (even the name suggests what was to come; it wasn't called Bowling Green Court) who played an uncompromising long ball game and battered teams into submission with mental and physical strength along with a huge self-belief born out of this approach.

Teams who came a cropper against Wimbledon would complain about the excess intimidation from the use of an extra loud ghetto blaster in the dressing room, to the high flying tackles and elbows of John Fashanu and Vinny Jones. This, in itself, was and still is, churlish because this excuse takes away the skill within the club from players such as Glyn Hodges who, as a winger and crosser of the ball, was second to none. I learned a great deal from him when we were at Watford together. There was a string of excellent players to emerge from Wimbledon and yet they never got the praise for their abilities, and many, such as Nigel Winterburn, Keith Curle and Terry Phelan went on to have super careers.

We suffered the same type of labelling, only it wasn't the type of play which the purists attacked, but our home pitch which was of course astro-turf, or as we called it 'Plastic.' Oldham Athletic had an advantage for sure at home because we were used to our pitch and it did spook many teams. The advantage we had was knowledge; how to play on it and we did it better than most even though the style of football it produced was the purest form ie. 'the passing game.' Most complaints were just sour grapes because teams got out-played and hadn't done their homework properly. Certainly our success was not matched by the three other teams which had plastic pitches: QPR; Preston North End; and Luton Town. Their records did not compare to ours. Quite simply we had some very good players and many went on to have excellent careers after their Oldham period was over.

Remarkably we had a few things in common with Wimbledon. We had a crazy outlook in the dressing room, we had talented players, we had unprecedented success and we were up against the football purists. What we didn't have in common was the philosophy of the game. The philosophy of the side, and hence the game, comes from the manager. In our case Joe Royle, who is without doubt a football purist and set up his team to play the passing game. This wasn't anything to do with us having a plastic pitch, it was his philosophy, formed no doubt as a player at Everton and it just made sense on such a surface. John Beck, incidentally a fan of the long ball game, tried to implement his long ball philosophy on the plastic pitch when he was the manager at Preston with disastrous results. Graham Taylor, the manager on the receiving end of the Aston Villa drubbing in the League Cup quarter-final (see later), was an exponent of the long ball game and he used it to great success at Watford, but he refused to blame the plastic pitch for his team's demise on the night.

Some fans can't get their heads around the origin of philosophy in football being manager related, but it really is the case. A football team represents the manager and what he wants and can even reflect a nation. The majority of fans in England like the frenetic 'Up and at you' approach compared to the cautious Italian retention of the ball and 'Catenaccio' formula or indeed the Argentine 'Gambeta' approach. The English Premier League has been likened to a bar room brawl by a leading Italian sports journalist, and was also compared to a game of chess which the Continentals prefer. Indeed, if a team begins to exhibit some ball retention in the English Premier League, it is not long before the crowd begins to lose patience and start baying for the ball to be clattered up the pitch.

The Brazilians have long dominated the world game with a combination of the long and short ball game, with a high degree of skill involved in both. If they hit it long it is a direct accurate pass not a lump into the channel, and an attempt to pick up the second ball, as we like to call it, in a game of physical roulette. In an interview with John Hartson on *Sky Sports,* he revealed absolutely what they had to do at Wimbledon. When the full backs got the ball they were instructed to hit the ball into the channel and under no circumstances to pass the ball to anyone else. Everyone on the team knew this and followed the philosophy through without argument. They bought into the manager's philosophy. If they didn't they would have been dropped!

Conversely, Joe wanted the full backs to pass the ball to the wingers as almost the first option at Oldham, but it was nowhere near as rigid as it was with Bobby Gould or Harry Bassett at Wimbledon. However, a failure to do this on a regular basis would result in a rebuke and even a substitution. So what does a manager look for when he wants to set up his side and implement his philophy or belief paradigm. You start with a belief or your philosophy, and then select players with strong personalities and characters to follow your plans. In order to do this they need the ability and desire to do so. Bonus characteristics are loyalty and intelligence. These two bonus characteristics are in short supply these days, especially loyalty, due to the nature of the industry and intelligence is purely luck.

Thus it follows logically that the personality of the manager is very important in order to attract players to sign up to his belief system. Joe Royle had just this, a sound and affable nature (still did the last time I spoke with him) and he had a tunnelled focussed belief which was to get into the top flight by playing a brand of attacking, passing football. Now that was a tall order! It is far easier, or was, to create success out of the long ball percentage game (also known as route-one football) than through a purist approach.

Finding the right players with the above ingredients was very difficult, especially for a small club like Oldham, as they had to compete with the wage structures of other clubs around the same league. Indeed finding a team at Oldham, packed with talent and strong personalities and with a strong collective desire was near on impossible and almost a fluke, but Joe did his research very well. It took him ten years to do it though but he never gave up on his principles. This couldn't happen now as managers don't get five minutes these days.

I know Joe did his homework on the personalities of players because prior to signing Redders he asked me for a character reference and I said, "Yes, he is mad enough to sign for us Gaffer!" That did it, and a day later he had joined the asylum. Joe could spot players and the entire squad seemed to be made up of misfit talent from big clubs, all with slightly different personalities. He did tell us all once that we were all at Oldham because there was something wrong with us and he was right. But Joe knew that he could deal with the strong and strange personalities and he helped channel our energies onto the pitch and watched our characters blossom. Some managers would never have put up with the stuff we did and would have cracked or come down too hard on us.

In the squad I joined in 1989 there was definitely something odd in the chemistry of the dressing room, and I began to instantly compare it to Watford. At Watford the players were all very serious minded compared to Oldham, it was the staff who were mad at Watford. The personnel gradually changed with the 14 games I selected but over time these lads proved they were all up to the task in hand.

Andy Rhodes was loud and in your face and loved to try to bully the kids with various orders and demands. Jon Hallworth was quiet but manically precise and tidy; he had his eye on everyone and quickly dished out any stick required for a particular situation. Denis Irwin was also very quiet but one sensed a slow fuse waiting to go off whilst Andy Barlow was simmering with aggression and, being the local boy, got a lot of stick but coped well with it. Redders used to do gorilla impressions of Andy by getting on all fours and walking around on his fists with his shorts in the crack of his backside. He would peel his lips back against his gums and grin at Andy and then leap up onto the bench beside him. Joe witnessed one of these cameos and walked out speechless.

Earl Barrett, Roger Palmer and Paul Warhurst were disturbingly quiet but Andy Holden was just clearly disturbed. Earl was only the subject of his feet, which were flatter than mine but any stick he received he just laughed along with, as indeed did Roger but nobody dare give Rodge any stick – how could you? I cannot either recall any racist comments at all during my footballing days playing alongside and against all skin colours and ethnic backgrounds and tolerance. The stick and humour was personal but not prejudice. It seems to have got worse now, perhaps due to media attention and a degeneration of humour, tolerance and sensitivity.

Mick Milligan (Sean O'Hooligan) was instantly recognisable as a nutter and was behind most of the practical jokes around the place. He was a pain in the backside on and off the field. Ian Marshall (Ogrond) was an annoyed scouser and always looked on the 'this is shit' side of things at most scenarios. He was fascinated by my feet, but he loved somebody else's poor predicament and would lay into them without mercy, whereas Nick Henry was somewhere between quiet and a menace, depending on the circumstances and how he felt.

Neil Adams was a constant noise in the background and a wind-up merchant. Andy Ritchie was affable and friendly but with a glint in his eye and had seen it all before. His strike partner Frankie Bunn was another silent assassin waiting to pounce on something in the background. Gary Williams was your typical dark horse who never missed a trick and was ready to seize on anybody's peculiarity. He was a cheeky chappy who kept his eye on everyone, didn't say much, but when he did it usually struck home. You hardly noticed Gaz. Scott McGarvey was a nice bloke who was a bit of a wise boy, which was funny as he was always telling the lads about money making schemes that never worked. Neil Redfearn had definitely got his eye on any chance to take the piss out of any situation and relate it to a real life simili.

Craig Fleming, nicknamed Norland (that's where he was from and is a typical Yorkshireman), started very quietly. I knew him from Halifax Town but he somehow developed a weird form of eccentricity as did Chris Makin, a quiet Mancunian who could bite fairly severely under pressure. Chris got endless stick about being a closet Manchester United fan. Richard Jobson was known as 007 due to his unflappable nature both on and off the pitch, and he never seemed to have a hair out of place – he was always man of the match too somehow. Graeme Sharp was quiet and found everything in the dressing room mildly amusing but never fully got the humour and we have already mentioned Neil McDonald.

Darren Beckford got christened 'Captain Dobbie' because of his big fat arse and was always getting shouted at by Joe for being lazy. Paul Moulden became known as 'Egga baka beans and a slice of two' because of his love of fry-ups; he was a cheeky chap and used to take the stick well. Neil Pointon was as loud as Rhodesy and used to drive us all mad with his war films on the bus and Paul Bernard was a genuinely quiet lad who somehow used to avoid any stick.

Gunnar Halle was quiet and didn't say much because of the language barrier but got nick-named 'Gruber' after *Banana Splits* which he knew nothing about being from Norway, but Redders let him know all right. Paul Kane was quiet and didn't attract any attention but was well liked and David Currie took everything in his stride but had a deep underlying sense of humour. Glynn Snodin was always laughing and a real pleasure around the place and again a typical Yorkie with his humour.

No matter what the sociological backgrounds and the different personality types, the boys who featured in these fourteen great games and all the other lads who played their part in the matches leading up to these tremendous events, were all great lads themselves and there wasn't a bad egg amongst them. This was down to Joe. He took the gamble and it paid off. He managed this bunch off misfits and created fame that Oldham hasn't known before or since. A special mention must go to his assistant Willie 'bad cop' Donachie who, at 38-years-old still played in the first team and was our fitness trainer, skills and drills trainer, and psychologist. He did really well with the former two but I am afraid he was at a loss with the psychology, although he did try – bless him! However, all this added up to a selection of characters on the field who all had genuine affection for each other and the manager, and I think it helped to pull us through situations that seemed lost.

Then there was the crowd at Oldham. I have said it before but I will say it again, I was shocked at the low attendances at Boundary Park when I first arrived in 1989. They had the second lowest, behind Oxford United, in the Second Division at just over the 6,000 mark. I can remember thinking that this was unsustainable for progression. We had to start winning to pull in the crowds, which is exactly what happened. By the end of the season, in the home game against Oxford following the League Cup Final, the crowd had doubled in size to over 12,000 regulars. Where did all these fans come from and where did they go? The simple answer is that I do not know but what I do know is that all the loyal fans, like Dave Moore, who have followed the club through bad and good times, and followed us around the country, and Europe, and travelled from the New World too, well this is your club. Keep making the noise of 20,000 and we were proud to play for you.

The Dressing Room

Jon Hallworth – Goalkeeper

Excellent shot stopper (well you should be being a keeper) and good with crosses – didn't get a lot wrong when coming for the ball in the air. He was very dedicated in training to a point of obsession which keepers have to be because of the isolated nature of their role. He used to get annoyed at me for shooting during crossing and shooting sessions as he used to steal ground in order to outwit the strikers during these practices, so I used to put him right. He was a very good talker and organizer and very quick to set up attacks with accurate distribution, both with kicks and throws. He was technically very good with the ball to his feet and brave when attacking players who had the ball at their feet. The save he made against John Sheridan during the latter stages of the Sheffield Wednesday game was a championship winning save, and a defining moment in his career. It is difficult writing about one of your best mates but he was a great goalie and apart from that a useless tw*t!

Andy Rhodes – Goalkeeper

Like 'Captain' an excellent shot stopper but more athletic with an elastic strength second to none. He used to lose his rag in training and chase people around the place who did him with a chip, although I cannot remember him ever catching anyone with his enormous expenditure of energy. He was not as gifted technically as 'Captain' with his feet, and his great performance in the League Cup Final was marred by an unlucky and ultimately mistimed one-on-one with Jemson for Forest's goal. Like Hallworth he was very brave to the point of fearless and definitely confirmed the analysis that most keepers are bonkers!

Denis Irwin – Full back

A two footed player with an excellent touch and appreciation of a pass. Flawless more-or-less all his career in defending because of his skills on the ball and pace off it. He was the start of the modern day wing-back with his relentless energy and drive and he formed a great partnership with Neil Adams on the right. Denis was a dead ball specialist and scored free-kicks and penalties with ease using the technique of top-spin with the instep which caused the ball to dip late. The action of top spin works well if you can generate high revolutions with the ball, which he could. His low centre of gravity allowed his small stature to recover against much bigger players and block their movements. An all-time Oldham great.

Andy Barlow – Full back
Tough and uncompromising with a massive engine, meaning he could go all day. He knew what he was good at and rarely put a foot wrong. Like me, he was not blessed with out and out pace but he more than made up for it with his ability to read the situation. His left foot was accomplished and he could cross a ball and had a good strike on him. He talked well to me and we got a good understanding together. He could hit the whole range of passes from diagonals to in-swingers and out-swingers. He would lay the ball off to me comfortably with the outside of his foot without breaking stride which gives the winger time. He has to be the best local player ever for Oldham and he coped well with the stick he copped.

Earl Barrett – Centre Half/Full back
Earl was a centre half primarily but could also play full back. However, he was not great technically in the way that Denis Irwin was. His distribution could be erratic from full back at times. At centre half he was almost impossible to get the better of and this was due to a combination of pace, endurance, strength, elasticity and his quick assessment of the situation. The number of times he bailed us out was so phenomenal that the Chaddy faithful used to sing *'You'll never beat Earl Barrett'* and not many did. He could also chip in with the odd goal which was a subtle side to his game. He received colossal stick about his feet and when he transferred to Aston Villa we presented a shoe box to Andy Gray, the Villa assistant manager saying, *'Can you give Earl his boots please, he left them?'* Contained within the box was a pair of flip-flops with studs pushed into them! It brought the Villa dressing room to a standstill with howls of laughter. Earl just smiled and shook his head.

Paul Warhurst – Centre Half/Full back

Paul was simply the quickest player in the land and certainly the quickest I had ever encountered. He was not a 'go in at all costs and win the ball' type which left him open to some criticism on occasions but he never used to have to in 99% of situations because his electric turn of speed would bail even Earl out. He was technically very gifted and proved what a great footballer he was when he eventually converted to a striker for Sheffield Wednesday later in his career. When Denis Irwin went to Manchester United we had a problem at right back, the loss of Den was a big blow to the club, but we needn't have worried as Paul filled the gap superbly.

Andy Holden – Centre Half

Injury blighted Andy's career and much of it was his own making because of his fearless approach. I don't think I have ever seen anyone go in as hard as 'Taff' did, especially in the air. I used to cringe at the noises I heard! He once, against Leeds, headed the back of Ian Baird's head and the ball acted like a billiard ball as it cannoned off Baird's head, off Taff's and went 60 yards. His dedication and determination to recover from injury will always live with me, and I still hold images of him in my mind, of him running up and down the terraces at Boundary Park with an apprentice under each arm as weights.

Ian Marshall – Centre Half/Centre Forward

One of my all-time favourite players, Marshy had everything. He had electric pace, incredible wiry strength and absolute aggression. He was superb in the air and a great finisher with both feet. He was a manager's dream on the pitch but off it he could be the manager's nemesis. Marshy had incredible timing at both heading and striking a ball and even when at full stretch seemed to get a sweet contact on the ball. At centre half he could move the ball out off his feet with such control that he didn't have to break stride to hit a massive 60 yard diagonal onto my chest with perfect back-spin. Marshy had a unique gift, the likes of which I haven't seen since, in that he was two players in one. He was brilliant in both defence and attack and this allowed Joe to make a substitution without taking anyone off the field. If he started at the back and we needed a goal he would just send him up front. If he started up front and we needed some security he would just drop him back into the back four. An incredible talent to have. How he never played for England is anyone's guess. I think I know why! He was an anti-establishment figure and his face didn't fit.

Mick Milligan – Midfield

'Indio' was another nickname I conjured for Milly and he also got called 'Donald Duck' at times too. These were both references to his character on the field. He was in short a menace and a thorn in the side for every team he played against. He was the annoying bandit, Indio, in midfield and would argue and get annoyed with us, the referee, and himself, like Donald Duck flapping his wings and protesting his innocence. What was he doing? Milly specialised in getting under everybody's skin. Joe called Milly and Nick Henry 'yard dogs' such was their ability to snap away at the opposition's attempt to gain mid-field control. His core skill was the ability to read the mind of the opposition and cut out through passes with incredible monotony. He must have made more interceptions than anyone in football. He seemed to lay traps and fool the opposing player into thinking he wasn't aware of what was going on. He had incredible spidery flexibility, and was also astonishingly good in the air for his size. When he got the ball he simply laid it off to me or Bert or whoever was available. He could also contribute with the odd goal from outside the box. I haven't seen a mid-fielder like him before or since.

Nick Henry – Midfield

Nick Henry, nicknamed 'Terry' in reference to his Scouse origins, was the other part of the yard dog duo in the middle of the park. Slightly smaller than Milly, he was every bit as tenacious and learned much from his slightly more experienced mate alongside him. He was a street fighter with an innocent body language. He had boundless energy and did more box-to-box running than his partner who tended to keep guard a little more. Consequently he scored the odd goal in the area but also contributed with some superb long range strikes. Again, like his mate, he was very effective with the ball once he won it, in that he didn't try to over-complicate things, he merely rolled it to a team mate. Nick had a tenacious element to him without getting annoyed at the referee or anyone else. He merely got on with his game and, for such a young lad, you would have thought that he had been playing where he did for a decade or more.

Neil Redfearn –Midfield

Another best mate so it's difficult to write about him. He will be forever remembered for the penalty which won Oldham's greatest ever prize – the Second Division Championship. He had incredible confidence and used to love winding the goalies up with trick finishes in training and would run off celebrating and laughing at the same time. I knew he would score the penalty and was the only man for the job in those circumstances. He knew he would score too. He was the best two footed player in the game at the time, and had a range of passing and shooting up there with any era. He could ping long passes out to the wingers with either foot and then he would be off down the middle, ready to pounce on any loose situations for a scoring chance. He wasn't blessed with blistering pace but that didn't matter. Redders had normous stamina and would win long distance runs by a mile, even leaving Earl in his wake. A true goal scoring midfielder, he would shoot from anywhere and his tally of 18 goals in the promotion year said it all. How he was overlooked by England when certain midfielders of the time got many caps is again beyond me. It smacks of a north/south divide as well as a prejudice against smaller clubs.

Neil Adams – Winger

A true wide man and an old fashioned winger but he could also play inside if asked to do so. He scored a similar ratio of goals to game as me, about one in seven, which is what wingers should do, but his major role of course was creating goals. Rapid over about ten yards and he had a very difficult to read in-to-out feint with just enough weight on the ball to enable a first time cross before the defender had recovered his balance. He could cut back and cross with his left foot, and was an excellent dead ball striker which was used effectively at corners and free kicks. It was important that we operated with two wingers when we could because this is how you can pull teams apart. Having Neil on the other wing would certainly help my game and I don't feel Joe played him enough at times. Certainly, in my opinion, he was a key player in many of Oldham's games, let alone the Great Games and he added a bit of mental steel to the team with his constant chipping away in the ears of the opposition – proper wind up merchant.

Frank Bunn – Forward

When I look at Bunny I think to myself, 'what did he have?' It is difficult to put a finger on a specific thing. Then it dawned on me that this is exactly what he was – it was that he did everything simply and effectively. He didn't particularly stand out because he did something magic, and he certainly didn't stand out because he made errors. He was the classic old fashioned centre forward who held the ball up and linked play, and then he got on the end to score a goal – simple. He unfortunately got injured and Oldham, and the football public, did not see enough of him. It was a real shame seeing him every morning as part of the dressing room chimp business, only to watch us all go out and play football whilst he was consigned to another mind-numbing gym session with Taff. That must have been heart breaking. The consolation was his never to be forgotten six goals against Scarborough which showed his class.

Andy Ritchie – Forward

Another best mate. Instantly fits into the category with Marshy and Redders who should have played for England, particularly when you considered who did in the same years. These may seem to be big statements but consider this; Andy Ritchie unhinged the best defences in the land, packed full of England players. The demolition of Arsenal by Andy in the League Cup in 1989/90 shows you what he was capable of. He was, in my opinion, the complete centre forward with an all-round game and deadly finishing to go with it. Even when he played in the Masters Football in the last decade he couldn't stop scoring. What were the skills he possessed? For a start he had vision and imagination, both for the pass and the goal. It was almost audacious and riddled with cheek the stuff he did! I never asked him about his approach although I did ask Roger about his insight, to which he just shrugged his shoulders. Both had though, an instinct to be at the right place at the right time. I didn't need to pick them out. I just crossed the ball and they were both there. This is instinct and thus you always had a chance of last gasp equalisers, like Southampton away. He had a great first touch and the ability to shield the ball whilst moving at the same time, which is a rare trick. He wasn't slow either but could dribble the ball and packed a lethal first time shot. His coolness in front of goal was another attribute and he improvised so well, like the goal when he rounded David James and back-heeled it in as he ran away from goal! I did ask him about his heading ability up against bigger centre halves, particularly from goal kicks, and his uncanny ability to win the ball. He used to stay well away from the centre half and at the last second when the defender thought he had it, Andy would appear from the side and jump across the lad and win the ball as it dropped. Very clever. The best player, arguably, in Latics History?

Roger Palmer – Forward

The record all-time goal scorer in Latics' history and he spent half of his time on the wing! As I mentioned previously about Andy, I once asked Rodge about his knack of being in the right place at the right time, all the time! He looked at me as if to say, 'What are you asking me a dumb arsed question like that for?' It was simple really, he just knew instinctively where to be. He had a funny way of kicking the ball sometimes but it still went in. He scored an absolute screamer away at Middlesbrough; playing on the right and cutting in onto his left foot he swept it into the top corner. It was the best strike I ever saw him do. He was blessed with electric movement, lots of pace, and above all he was very brave. He wrote so many players off in one-on-one situations, to which I didn't even bother enquiring as to if it was calculated! Quite simply he was a phenomenon and the fans still sing 'Ooooh Roger Palmer' to this day, and will rightly always be remembered for his Oldham career – a legend.

Gunnar Halle – Midfield/Full back

Gunnar was from Norway or, as I coined, from Norwhere! He just turned up one day and we all thought, 'Who the hell is this?' I assumed he was bought to replace Denis Irwin. Certainly we had never heard of him as foreign players were exceptions in the pre *Sky TV* domination years. If he turned up today nobody would bat an eyelid. Naturally he was shy and quiet as he spoke little English and had just joined a mad house, poor lad. It didn't take Redders long to christen him 'Gruber' because of his slight bucked teeth, but of course he hadn't a clue what the reference was. He took it in his stride and soon began to put a useful mark on the squad. It is difficult to pin-point his exact skills but he was 'Mr Consistent' whether operating in midfield, full back or on the right wing. He had a massive engine and would cover every blade of astro-turf and, like Milly and Nick, was a yard dog and loved a tackle on astro turf. I can recall his pale white skin around his knees always being bloody, such was his commitment. He could contribute to creating and scoring goals but in his first years at Oldham he was plagued by injury. He was a popular well liked lad.

Richard Jobson – Centre Half

Jobbo, or 007, was a rock in the heart of our defence and rarely had a bad game. He was coolness personified and unflappable. He never had a hair out of place after heading the ball all afternoon. In fact, he caused me to ask Joe who picked the man of the month every time to which he replied, *"I do!"* I asked why Jobbo won it every time and why I never won it in all my fifty months at the club. Joe avoided the answer but said that I was always a close second. I protested that I needed the clothes vouchers from *Lou's Menswear* more than Jobbo did but to no avail. So 007 was a consistent steady, no nonsense act who never seemed to miss a header or a game for that matter. He was a tremendously strong athlete and it was difficult to get the better of him in training. He was tidy on the ground without being flash, but he was a refined Andy Holden lacking only the injuries that Andy picked up. His biggest asset was in the air, particularly from attacking set pieces, and there was a stage where I deliberately aimed for him at corners and he contributed with many goals from this tactic. A very underrated player in his time but obviously not by Joe!

Graeme Sharp – Forward

I remember being at home in Skipton, listening to the radio, when it was announced that Oldham had made a big signing. I was excited at this but never expected it to be as big a name as this. He was a First Division giant and top class centre forward. An expert at his job which was leading the line, bullying centre halves and referees and scoring goals. Of course he had to be to play for Everton, following such greats as Dixie Dean, Joe Royle, Bob Latchford and Andy Gray. I knew him, we all did, from our previous encounters against Everton and I didn't need to ask him any dumb questions as to his 'ways' as it was plain to see. In my opinion he did a great job for us in his time on the pitch because he was constantly carrying a bad back. He job-shared with Andy Ritchie quiet a lot, which was a clever move by Joe, for our first year in top flight football. To me, his abilities were strength in holding the ball up, strength in the air and strength of character. He brought us experience. The two goals he scored against Manchester City away said it all about him – first rate.

Neil Pointon – Full back

You could not Neil call shy like Gunnar, in fact he was the opposite. He was noisy and confident which he carried onto the pitch. This didn't mean he wasn't a nice lad and I know that he had a sensitive nature as he expressed to me recently when I spoke to him. He was a good full back who did his job with full commitment to Oldham and never gave up a situation. His determination helped him to score two goals in consecutive FA Cup semi-finals, and not many people can say that. He came from Manchester City via Everton in an exchange deal for me, along with Steve Redmond. He again brought experience to Oldham's first year in the Premier League. I didn't get to know him as well as Andy Barlow and I often found it frustrating to play with him as he would be keen to hit a big diagonal pass to Sharpy instead of giving the ball to me. That is how the dynamics of teams change. Nonetheless, a good signing by Joe and he was always willing to get forward from left back.

Paul Kane – Midfielder

Paul joined us from Aberdeen, basically as cover for the run in to getting promotion to the old First Division. It was a shrewd acquisition by Joe but fortunately (and this is not meant in a bad way) we didn't need to use him much as we thought we would as the anticipated injuries and loss of form just did not occur. He was a nice genuine lad who contributed to our success in the run in to promotion, as well as the early games of the following season. I can't really say that I saw him play enough to make much of an assessment.

Craig Fleming – Centre Half

Craig came to us from Halifax Town. The rest of the lads hadn't heard of him but I had, having been at Halifax myself and having played with his elder brother Paul. They were chalk and cheese in build as Paul was essentially a dwarf, and Craig was a mountain. Norland as he got nicknamed because of his quaint insistence when asked where he came from always answered, *"NORLAND,"* in a big deep Yorkshire accent, as if anybody knew where that was? If he had said Halifax (Norland is a small village up in the hills of Halifax) then the lads might have heard of it. As I mentioned Craig was big and strong, fearless and lightning quick. At 14 it is rumoured that he was playing reserve team football at Halifax, and he certainly slotted straight into Oldham's set up and quickly established himself as a first team player in the top flight. The job he did on Mark Hughes in the FA Cup semi-final at Wembley was magnificent and showed he could mix it with anyone. I am surprised that he didn't get snatched up by a big club but he eventually followed Milly and Bert into the wilderness that is Norwich. From Norland to Norfolk via Oldham.

Scott McGarvey – Forward

Scott reminded me of my Uncle Ken who played for Burnley and Tranmere and who also had a spell in the US carnival with Chicago Sting in the first coming of soccer in the United States. By this, I mean he was from another era in the way he spoke and his mannerisms. 'The boy this…' 'the big man…' 'the wee fella…' it amused me and captivated me. He was old world from Glasgow and played for Manchester United in 1980 as a 17-year-old. He was another Scottish acquisition by Joe who was brought in to provide cover and experience. He didn't play much but he showed enough flashes in training to convince me that he was once was a very good player. I warmed to him and I know he liked me. On nights out I always ended up in his company and loved listening to his wise-boy schemes and his olde worlde football speak!

David Currie – Forward

David joined us from Nottingham Forest and I knew him to be a very exciting player with skills I admired and aspired to – that of dribbling the ball and taking men on. He had a lovely left foot. I have always loved this style of play and grew up thinking I was Mario Kempes and so did Doddy judging by his hairstyle. He joined us as cover in the run-in to the end of the promotion season. It was Joe's attempt to buy every forward in the league. To be fair it was a good idea with Bunny being injured, Andy prone to injury and carrying a bad back, and Marshy needed for defensive cover as we were thin on the ground. Doddy scored a great goal against Sheffield Wednesday at Hillsborough in that monster game which was watched by 35,000. The goal typified him latching on to a through ball and rounding the keeper to score from an acute angle. He was an extremely amusing man off the field without realising it and was another regular victim for Redders, Milly and Marshy! He exasperated Joe, most centre forwards did, and he wasn't shy of answering back with the odd witticism.

Paul Bernard – Midfield

Paul was only 17 and playing just his second game for the first team when he scored that all-important equaliser against Sheffield Wednesday to win glory for Oldham. What maturity, but then again he was a strong lad and burst through the maximum sit-ups bleep test of 20/20 without breaking a sweat while we were all cramped up on 12/20. He was in a similar vein to Gunnar Halle, in that he was very competent and full of running, but yet not spectacular. He never copped for any stick which might have pointed to the biggest insult (boring) but I think that it points to the fact that we all knew that he was the kid, and we therefore looked after him and left him alone. He played a couple of times for Scotland but sadly injury curtailed his career. I don't have a clue what he is doing now sadly.

Glynn Snodin – Full back

Glynn joined us from Leeds United at the start of the big time in the old first division and was a bit of a surprise signing as far as I was concerned. Then again, he was a loan signing and was probably brought in as cover for Andy Barlow in addition to bringing in some experience. I played about eight games with him, and a very good player he was too. That shows as it only took a few games to work that out. He was a nice lad but his stay was short lived.

Gary Williams – Winger

Gary was a tidy player and no slouch on the wing. He didn't get much chance to shine because of me and Bert doing jobs out wide. He was our Mick Bates – always the substitute but did a reliable job when required. He loved the banter and the famous incident that stands out is his castigation of Peter Reid in a pub in Manchester. Reidy had a few on board and took exception to us all enjoying ourselves and made comment to the tune that, 'We hadn't won anything yet' type of thing. Gaz was awoken from his malaise and said in his West Country accent, *"Oh, I remember you, chasing that Maradona with your flip flops on!"* Reidy went mad and left the scene.

Neil McDonald – Full back

Neil made a funny kind of start at Oldham, but nevertheless became a well like and valued member of Oldham's squad and he featured in 14 Great Games, like Sharpy, for and against us with Everton. He was strong and a good passer of the ball and did have experience. Although his cock-ups undoubtedly helped us in the Everton trilogy, he got christened a 'double agent.' He didn't hit it off with our coach Willie Donachie and I can remember some heated exchanges, centring on his weight and fitness in Willie's new training regimen. As a player he was good shall we say, and had an influence at Oldham in the few games he played, but his exchanges revealed something to me which has been borne out since. He was dead keen on coaching and managing and has proved that by going on to have an excellent coaching career, so far-fair play to 'Roaring Thunder Heed.'

Willie Donachie – Player/Assistant Manager

Willie was and is a one-off that is for sure. To be fair, as we like to say in football, he was the most experienced person in this whole 14GG period. He had, after all, played in the 1978 World Cup Finals in Argentina and had been part of Manchester City's league championship side of 1968. He was by far the most experienced and wise man of us all. Even Joe hadn't played in a World Cup – how could he? He was English after all. I will be honest that at first, and at last, I found him an inspirational man and coach. He believed in me and told me that I would make the difference to this team. I was a bit non-plussed by this but he inspired me without doubt. I connected with him. I knew who he was and asked him stuff that I couldn't ask other people. Like what was it like playing against Jairzinho? How did you stop Jairzinho? The answer was simple he said, *"Against someone as quick as him, I had to drop deep to stop him running in behind me and force them to give the ball to his feet, so at least I could see where he was!"* Simple but effective and Willie brought this pragmatism to our teams. Willie was less tolerant than Joe with regards to the schoolboy/university humour and if he detected any 'pissingabooot' as he put it, in training he would often lose his rag and we would be running!

He hated losing more than anyone I have ever met and would be really annoyed if he lost a game of head tennis. He was so delighted when we won that he would go around the dressing room and shake everybody's hand after the game and sit down and talk to individuals about their performances. In terms of preparation for games he would leave 'no stone unturned' so we knew what we were up against and what to do about it. He led by example by keeping himself immaculately fit which allowed him to still play first team football in our team of stars. Sometimes his methods were a little bit odd and this led to some hilarious moments on the training ground. Here is the funniest – he was trying to make a point about communication in a large and packed stadium before we were due to play at one, say Maine Road, and said that you can hear a lot more than you think out there. He had us gathered around in a large circle on little Wembley (our training ground) and said, *"Shut up and listen,"* in his Glaswegian accent. After a minute or so of compliance in which, to be honest, I could hear the M62 motorway traffic in the background and birds singing in nearby trees, he said, *"What can you hear?"* As soon as those words left his lips Marshy farted, and it was a proper 'verumph' fart which collapsed the entire circle into fits of uncontrollable laughter and totally ruined poor Willie's point about being aware of things around you. He was exasperated and walked off the training ground swearing and shaking his head leaving Joe to finish off the session! Willie was a crucial and often forgotten main cog in our success, and his contribution to all our careers was vital. He was a top bloke and still is and he was recently appointed as assistant manager at Hartlepool United.

Ian Liversedge – Physiotherapist

Ian had a great sense of humour and handled the lads very well. He was well liked and essentially one of the lads himself. He had his off the field moments and that endeared him even more to us. He inspired me to go on to be a physiotherapist and we all had a lot of time for him.

Ronnie Evans – Kitman

Unlike any kitman in the world he actually like giving the lads gear. Most kitmen resent doing that and tend to hoard the stuff. Again he was well liked and formed a double act with 'Soss' the phsyio, especially on away trips – Friday nights out! Super bloke.

Jim Cassell – Chief Scout

Jim was a botanist and he even looked like one but he could spot a player. He was a lovely bloke who knew his onions and was responsible for heading up the unique set of players that Oldham managed to get. He was understated and under-rated, but not by us.

Billy Urmson – Coach

Loud as 'Foook' but what a nice fellow. Brought the yard dogs on from youth level and was always on hand to help anybody. Great to have around the place and often subject of practical jokes by players and management. I once set fire to his jumper on the Isle of Man in the Central Pub (he wasn't wearing it at the time) and he thought it was hilarious until he realised it was his! I bought him a replacement Peel Golf Club jumper the next day.

Rick Holden 2015

Oldham v Leeds – League Cup Second Round 1989/90 2-1

Tuesday 19th September 1989
Boundary Park 7:30pm

OLDHAM		LEEDS
Andy Rhodes	1	Mervyn Day
Dennis Irwin	2	Mel Sterland
Andy Barlow	3	Michael Whitlow
Nick Henry	4	Vinnie Jones
Ian Marshall	5	Chris Fairclough
Earl Barrett	6	Peter Haddock
Roger Palmer	7	Gordon Strachan
Andy Ritchie	8	David Batty
Frank Bunn	9	Ian Baird
Mike Milligan	10	Bobby Davison
Rick Holden	11	John Hendrie
Gary Williams	12	Gary Williams
Paul Warhurst	14	Noel Blake
Manager: Joe Royle		Manager: Howard Wilkinson

Referee: RA Hart (Darlington). Linesmen: JA Perry (Bootle);
BM Rice (Wirrall).

Crowd: 8,415

Of course I can remember lots of detail about all the games I played in for every club but it is always handy to look back at programmes to check the finer points. That is, of course, until you look at Oldham Athletic memorabilia and find it all to be wrong! Well I might exaggerate but the Leeds programme was littered with errors such as failing to acknowledge my goals against Watford and Plymouth at home and even getting the score wrong against Plymouth putting us down for a 2-1 victory when in fact we won 3-2. Interestingly enough there is an aggressive copyright statement at the bottom of the statistics page saying that, *'These fixtures are the copyright of the Football League Ltd and are not to be reproduced without permission.'* Well you wouldn't want to!

We had made a shaky start to the season but personally I was flying, having scored three goals and created a few, including one in particular against Swindon which rescued a point at home. This was a particularly funny goal because I received the pass to create the goal off Osvaldo Ardiles, the great Argentine international World Cup winner from 1978 who was player manager for Swindon – he was mortified! We were going nowhere and he had possession of the ball but his intended pass went straight to me and I just whipped the ball in for Roger Palmer to score. It was comical for us and tragic for him. Even greats can get it wrong!

So we approached this League Cup game not in the best of form though personally I was full of confidence at my new club. I had made a great start to my Latics career and the crowd seemed to warm to my style of play and stupid goal celebrations. Leeds would be tough, we knew that, because they wanted promotion back to the top flight and under Howard Wilkinson; they were a well organized machine and had invested in people like Vinnie Jones to give them the traditional Leeds bite!

Their starting line up was Mervyn Day in goals, Mel Sterland at right back marking me, and Mike Whitlow at left back. Two centre halves were Chris Fairclough and Peter Haddock. The midfield four were, David Batty and Vinnie in the middle with John Hendrie on the left and Gordon Strachan on the right. Up front were Ian Baird and Bobby Davison. It was a solid looking team and one which would go on to get promotion! They were tough down the spine with Iain Baird being a particular handful, and David Batty and Vinnie were their menacing selves and the whole side was at this time orchestrated by the diminutive but hugely respected Gordon Strachan with whom I was later to have an amusing run in with when I was at City!

I am, it is well documented, a Leeds fan – growing up in the seventies in Yorkshire you could only be a Leeds fan as they were hugely talented and successful although they didn't win nearly half as much as they should have, due largely to bad luck in my opinion, but then again I am biased! There was a tension in the ground because of the Leeds fans and their Mongolian behaviour which had in recent seasons been exacerbated by some very close games and cross border Lancashire/Yorkshire rivalry. In fact when we finally overcame Leeds in the second leg at Elland Road it would be the third time Oldham had knocked them out of the cup in four years which didn't amuse the Peacocks fans!

The crowd was large for Oldham and later reported to be 8,415 of which many were mates supporting Leeds, and I could see them behind the goal at the Rochdale Road end glaring at me as I warmed up. I avoided eye contact and tried to concentrate on my preparation for the game which, when you play against the team you support, is not easy because you have odd thoughts going through your head. It is all right once you kick off but beforehand every player will tell you that it is a strange situation. You are so determined to play well to impress them and sometimes you can try too hard and get too wound up and let yourself down. If you score how do you celebrate? The thing is you have to be 100 percent professional because you are representing your club and your fans and you are an employee after all, so all thoughts have to be put to one side.

The game started at a furious pace and we tried to get on top. Our midfield of Mick Milligan and Nick Henry were easily a match for Batty and Jones as destroyers and the tussles cancelled each other out for a while. I wasn't getting much service as a consequence. Then on 27ish minutes, the best bit of skill that I have ever seen Vinnie do resulted in a Strachan goal, which he took really well. Vinnie unhinged us with a lovely backheel which released Strachan into the area and he hit a low first time shot past Rhodesy. Part of the problem was that we didn't expect this from Vinnie and Joe had made us a bit complacent with him by saying, "*if Vinnie gets the ball make an angle*" which was a bit disparaging if funny, but the fact remains that his thuggery and aggressive personality portrayed as a no-nonsense East End gangster later made reality in his movie career with *Lock, Stock and Two Smoking Barrels.* It over-shadowed his skill which he did possess. Okay he was no Maradona but he was a professional footballer and a winner, and had skills that had not to be underestimated – which we did! So we had to get a grip.

Shortly afterwards a move down our left resulted in a throw in to us. Andy Barlow quickly lobbed it into Frank Bunn at the right hand corner of the box. He was surrounded by four Leeds players but he played a beautiful ball around the corner for Andy who had made a superb little sideways bit of movement. Suddenly, released Andy who was coming into the form of his life, pushed the ball onto his right foot and from about 20 yards out he smashed the ball into the left hand corner of the net at the Chaddy End. Gordon Strachan could only watch as the ball screamed in to the net. He didn't curl the ball, it was hit more with top spin which he used to practice doing in training. This is a technique which he perfected in order to keep long range shots down. Balls were becoming lighter all the time and we had all worked it out that we had to keep the thing low, especially at Boundary Park, so that the bounce would make a low shot either skid or skip up slightly and freak the keeper. As it was, Mervyn Day was well beaten and the Chaddy End went mad!

It was the start of a revolution from the terraces in terms of singing and they eventually became part of the team. I remember vividly the lighters and the cigarettes flaring in the crowd which was 6,000 people in the one stand. It is of course ruined now by the 'all seater stadia' fiasco and the crowd does not generate the same atmosphere as it did back in the day, which is a real shame. Actually it is not a real shame it's an absolute scandal, because all it needed was to be a properly monitored standing area to prevent overcrowding and to provide proper escape routes onto the pitch to avoid crushing, but I digress!

I can't recall why Joe Royle decided to pick the side he did and he would have to ring Neil Adams, or Bert as we called him, as he was left out of the team and Roger Palmer played wide right instead. Looking at it as logically as I can it may have been that Joe was really playing three up front, or even four if you count me. He probably thought that with Marshy, Earle, Dennis and Andy Barlow, as well the two terriers, Milly and Nick behind us, that he had enough defensive cover to cope with Leeds and just let the four front men get on with it! Certainly it was a front four capable of scoring goals. Andy Ritchie was as prolific as at any time in his career and Frankie Bunn was entering the form of his life. We all knew that Roger Palmer could score in a dark room and you would only know he was there if he flashed his teeth; and myself, well I had started to score goals early in the season and could chip in. I always fancied myself as a centre forward and took a pride in being the best finisher in the club when we had training sessions involving finishing. My job, however, was to create goals which I loved doing. It was a lethal side and, when I look back now, no wonder teams struggled to cope with us.

One problem however was service, which at times dried up during this game. This was due to the midfield melee going on from both sides. The two teams did not really display lots of width on the night which stifled the game. For Leeds, Strachan was playing as a winger tucked in on the right and Hendrie was playing on the left, both unnatural positions for them. Strachan was a central midfielder doing a job out right but he would naturally tuck inside. With Hendrie being right footed he would come inside rather than look to stretch Dennis Irwin down the flank. Roger Palmer was a centre forward and so it was only me, of the four wide men on the night, playing in my normal position. This made the game compact.

It was, ironically, the reason that I scored the goal I did just before half time, because I got frustrated and came in off the line looking for the ball. I can't recall exactly what happened but the ball was clattered down the middle and bounced off one of their players to me and I decided to go on a run. I liked doing that and, although lots of coaches used to despair when the runs broke down, it never stopped me trying as it often took sides by surprise when I did it.

My crazy goal celebration after netting against the team I supported

I managed to weave my way past Batty and Sterland and, as I entered the box, big Noel Blake clipped me and I started to go down. It would have been a penalty for sure but a bit of brilliant refereeing saved the day. Mervyn Day hesitated and I am convinced for the only reason that he thought a penalty was going to be given and that I couldn't possibly reach the ball. But in that moment I stuck out my left foot and slid it past him. The ref had played a brilliant advantage. It was almost like a goal by default. But it went in and the Chaddy End went bananas again – it went to 2-1 and we were flying.

The second half followed the same midfield congested pattern as the first, but Leeds were the more likely to score an equalizer than we were to grab a third. We just couldn't get going. It had been like that all season and when I say all season, it was early days I admit, but we hadn't really got going. Joe hadn't quite got the balance right because in my opinion, if you are going to play 4:4:2 in the conventional sense then you need two natural wingers who both enjoy playing wide. One winger is often not enough to stretch teams. Roger was simply not a winger, brilliant player that he was, and our two fullbacks, Dennis and Andy, did not get forward and wide often enough to become wing-backs because they were preoccupied with defending a tight unit. Joe, in my opinion, encouraged Dennis and Andy to get forward later in the season but not during this game. Because of the narrow nature of both midfields they were tucked in protecting the centre halves. Leeds came close on a couple of occasions but Rhodesy in goal was up to it and saved us a couple of times and towards the end I should have scored with a long range effort but just got underneath it slightly and it hit the bar.

Still we were buzzing in the dressing room afterwards because it was a good performance and we thought solely that it would help our league form. There was absolutely no thought of cup glory at this time. Why would there be? Our next game was against West Bromwich Albion at home in four days time and we needed to beat them to get up the league. I for one wanted to get back in the First Division to experience the heady days that I had at Watford in the top flight. None of us wanted to be playing Second Division football but that is what we were doing. There is little point dwelling on the second leg at Elland Road because it is not one of the games that I have chosen to highlight. What we eventually achieved is worth mentioning as is the point that Andy Ritchie and Frankie Bunn underlined their absolute class with two superb goals which saw poor old Leeds off 2-1. We were on our way!

Amusing Anecdote 1: The anecdote surrounding this game is regarding my grandpa, who was an avid football fan and supported Burnley for his sins and could never get his head around the fact that I became a professional footballer. He viewed footballers as Gods and to have his grandson as one troubled him somewhat! He was in fact a very good all round sportsman himself and played more or less everything from cricket to golf, bowls, football and all the indoor stuff like snooker and darts, and even dominoes. I never beat him at snooker, even when he was in his mid-eighties, and you had to watch him with an assiduity when playing dominoes because he would play wrong ones!

He visited every race ground for both dogs and 'hosses' in the North and was a compulsive gambler, or should I say betting man, and he was always astute. He taught me reverse betting for emotional comfort. This involves betting on the team you don't want to win so that if it comes off you're in the money but if you lose you are delighted for your team. So what all the Oldham fans should do every week is put the money on the opposition to win or draw and you can't lose. He actually ran an illegal bookies from the back of his newsagents shop in Colne for many a year.

He loved a tipple and went out on the pop every day from 1945, when he got back from the war, until he died in 2001 aged 88; drinking himself into an early grave! This behaviour caused many hilarious moments and I could write a separate book on the topic but one incident at Leeds was particularly amusing. In the return leg of this tie at Elland Road he got there early and went into the Peacock pub opposite the ground. He immediately started consternation by telling all the Leeds fans that Oldham were going to win and, as was his wont, he told them to put their money where their mouths were! They took a dim view of this but because he was an old bloke they didn't action any violence and it just became banter. Now, he had an ability also to worm his way into any social scene and always got himself into the top bars of any sporting occasion with his repartee – Leeds United was no exception, so during the game he was in the executive lounge. He managed to get himself locked outside in the main stand during the final throws of the game by taking a wrong turning; in order to get back in at the final whistle after our triumph he started banging on the door. The door was opened eventually by the landlord of the Peacock pub who was an executive member of the club, he was greeted by my grandpa who held his hand out for his money and said 'told you so!' What chance did I have with antecedents like this? Funny as you can get!

At the time of this game the fans were still steadying themselves for the start of another new season. Every season begins the same for the fans, along with the sometimes greatly inflated high expectations, the hope of promotion, fears of relegation and the wish of drawing some decent teams for cup-runs to bring a few bob in; the usual excitement of yet another upcoming journey into the unknown which would undoubtedly bring the anticipated highs and lows that were to follow.

Joe Royle was still slowly establishing himself as manager after taking over from long serving Latics fans' favourite, Jimmy Frizzell. It took a very long time for the fans to stop chanting for 'Sir' Jimmy but they were finally warming to 'Big Joe' who was building a team which would eventually become an amazing outfit, admittedly built from other teams cast-offs combined with his uncanny nouse of spotting the rough diamond at the right price; these would eventually become part of an exceptional collection of fine jewels, the Royle collection, which would be envied by supporters from all over the country.

The previous season had seen Athletic finish in the bottom half of the table in sixteenth place. They had been knocked out of the FA Cup at the first hurdle and had reached a third round replay before succumbing to Everton in the League Cup. Who could have predicted what was about to happen in the coming season? It was beyond all reasoning but will unfold as these 14 games are recollected.

Joe Royle's pre-match programme notes stated, *'Welcome back to Boundary Park for the visit of our 'inevitable' opponents from Yorkshire, Leeds United. We could be forgiven for thinking that our clubs were allotted magnetic tokens for when the draw was made if one considers the number of times we have played each other in recent seasons.'*

C A.F.C. BOUNDARY PARK, OLDHAM

REA | CHADDERTON ROAD
(COVERED TERRACE)

LEEDS UNITED F.C.
TUESDAY 19TH SEPTEMBER 89
KICK-OFF 7:30PM
LITTLEWOODS CUP
SECOND ROUND

You are advised to take up your position half an hour before the kick-off.

FOR TICKET AND MATCH INFORMATION TELEPHONE
061-624 4972
(24 HR. SERVICE)

ADULT
£ 4.00
(inc. VAT)

SECRETARY.

585

TO BE RETAINED

Match Ticket – excellent value for money at the time

This particular game began as the usual run-of-the-mill League Cup game against highly fancied Leeds United, and one which supporters would not have batted an eyelid at had they got knocked out as all the neutrals expected. The game itself was an inauspicious affair; this was the third meeting of the clubs in this particular competition in four seasons. Both clubs were Second Division teams and had battled out league games also but this match was full of incidents and was quite a tough fought affair.

The opening goal by Strachan was one to be cherished, and was laid on by that bit of magic from bad-boy Vinny Jones. At one stage Leeds' Bobby Davison careered head first into the perimeter fence at the Chaddy End .... I think some of the Oldham faithful were suggesting that the only way would be to get the fire brigade summoned to extricate his noggin from the railings! Former leeds man Andy Ritchie levelled for the home side before 'our' Rick stumbled through numerous tackles to slide the winner home. However, the final result was well deserved and showed the fighting spirit of the team; it also gave them a slender lead to take back to Elland Road for the second leg.

However, the first leg result was suitably celebrated in the pub after the final whistle had been blown. In the return leg at Elland Road, one of the Oldham fans reckoned that both of our goals might have been a fraction offside but admitted that, even so, they were both well put away by Bunn and Ritchie. It didn't matter anyway as we were through to the next round with a 4-2 aggregate score. Very few of the 8,415 people who witnessed this match could have imagined what was to unfold in the upcoming nine months. What would the draw for the second round bring?

Oldham v Scarborough – League Cup Third Round 1989/90 7-0

Wednesday 25th October 1989
Boundary Park 7:30pm

OLDHAM		SCARBOROUGH
Andy Rhodes	1	Ian Ironside
Dennis Irwin	2	Alan Kamara
Andy Barlow	3	Christian Short
Nick Henry	4	Paul Olsson
Paul Warhurst	5	Steve Richards
Earl Barrett	6	Ian Bennyworth
Neil Adams	7	Paul Dobson
Andy Ritchie	8	Tommy Graham
Frank Bunn	9	Steve Norris
Mike Milligan	10	Paul Robinson
Rick Holden	11	Martin Russell
Willy Donachie	12	Steve Saunders
Gary Williams	14	Gary Brook
Manager: Joe Royle		Manager: Colin Morris

Referee: JE Martin (Alton). Linesmen: J Hilditch (Stoke); D Orrell (Wigan).

Crowd: 7,712

The thing that still stands out in my mind after all these years is the reaction of the Scarborough players and management on TV after they had drawn us! A film crew had them all in the dressing room awaiting their fate because there was massive interest in them, having triumphed over Chelsea in the previous round. That in itself was a remarkable achievement to say the least because Chelsea were a First Division club and to come out on top over two legs against that calibre of opposition is rare. In one-off games anything can happen but over two games it meant, quite clearly, that Scarborough were no mugs!

Anyway when they were pulled out second to face us there was a collective groan from all their players and officials alike – it was clearly a big disappointment to be drawn against 'little' Oldham Athletic and I can understand why because we were not household names yet, merely a northern mill town with a steady unfashionable history. I can remember thinking 'the cheeky bastards' and thought we will hammer these for that, though I didn't quite expect the outcome to be as it did turn out!

I was perhaps the only player on our team who had had first-hand experience against Scarborough because I had played against them a couple of years or so earlier for Halifax Town. It was a tough team then built in the Neil Warnock tradition and though he had left for pastures new by the time Oldham were to play them, I expected them to be resilient if nothing else. When I played for Halifax up at Scarborough I had a particularly tough time against the full back, Alan Kamara, a relation of Chris Kamara who now features on *Sky Sports,* hyped up about the weekend's action. Kamara had marked me like a limpet all afternoon and I was desperate to do something telling in the game because I had missed the team bus along with my fellow student-player Frank Harrison, and we had to drive up to Scarborough behind the team bus.

Billy Ayre, the manager, was not amused and, as we were one nil down, a bollocking was coming my way. So in the end I had to go to the other wing (the right) where, thankfully, I crossed a ball for Russell Black to score. Kamara followed me as he had been told to man mark me regardless of whether I went for a shit or not, but he didn't think I would cross the ball with my right foot but I cut outside and crossed it with my right foot; they were undone. I learned much from that game! I therefore knew what to expect from him when we played them in this cup tie. Only two other players survived from the Scarborough team of two years earlier: Ian Bennyworth, a centre half, and goal scoring midfielder Tommy Graham. I knew of Tommy because of his links with Halifax Town where he was to return shortly after this game.

The game started rapidly with us putting Scarborough under severe pressure and it only took ten minutes to score our first goal. It was an easy tap in for Frankie Bunn after a cross that I had slid in, with the outside of my left foot, which had caused chaos for the back four and the keeper. I had by now started to work out what type of crosses and from where, would cause maximum confusion on the plastic pitch and an early low one often did the trick. The second goal on 18 minutes was a far simpler affair and down chiefly to bad marking. Neil Adams was playing, which I was very pleased about, and his corner to the back stick was powered in by Frankie almost unopposed. I sensed Scarborough had gone by now anyway but it was no time to relax. Those groans and jeers were still in the back of my mind and I wanted to make them know who we were.

Just two minutes later Andy Ritchie was tackled as he tried to go around the keeper on the right edge of the six yard box and the ball squirmed out to me on the left and I just swivel crossed it without looking into the box. I had no idea who was there but might have guessed as Frank came steaming in and smashed it side foot, to the keepers left. Hat-trick for Bunny and game over after just 20 minutes! Poor old Scarborough had been the unwitting victims of something that was to prove amazing in a very short space of time. You could see their deflated body language and you just knew it could be a cricket score. Joe had warned us not to take it lightly and I certainly wasn't going to against Mr Kamara after my previous encounter with him, but on the night I never saw him at all as he seemed to be playing left back with the number two shirt on!

This was the start of everything we wanted to achieve as a team, which was to play high tempo football and blow teams away. If we got at teams early they would crumble and lose their defensive shape but I still maintain that we were at our most effective when we stretched teams with our wide men and Neil Adams was key to this because he was a natural wide man. Neil Redfearn was posted out on the right at times but he clearly didn't want to be there and often protested to Joe and this was ultimately why he left the club at the end of the 1990/91 season. I also feel that is the reason why we didn't achieve promotion in 1989/90. Frank's fourth goal was a good finish when he was put through by Milly after they had lost possession, and he ran in almost unopposed towards goal simply because they had clearly gone at this stage. However, the fifth goal is what I am talking about regarding natural wingers and full backs willing to overlap. Dennis and Andy were always ready to get past their wingers with Andy sometimes doing too much to my liking! Bert had the ball and drew inside allowing Dennis to overlap and put a good cross in for Bunny to score at the near post – simple. Five nil at half time and it could have been more!

At half time Joe was pleased that we hadn't taken them lightly and could realise his promise to the fans in the match day programme to get into the hat for the next round for a change, and try to put a cup run together. It was ironic that we did just that in both competitions but it also contributed to our failure in the league to get into the play-offs. In the second half Scarborough defended more resolutely overall but quickly succumbed to the goal of the game by Andy Ritchie. This was classic route-one stuff, with a kick from Andy Rhodes and a flick on from Bunny. I can remember taking a chance on the left side of Bunny whilst Andy gambled on the right side. He let the ball run past him which turned the defender who got too tight. This is what you don't do to a quality striker because he just rolls you. The ball sat up perfectly for Andy to volley it from twenty yards into the roof of the net. It overshadowed any of Frank's goals but Frank went on to have the last say by claiming his sixth goal.

This was a beautifully worked goal and one which happened often on the Boundary Park surface. This time in was Andy Barlow breaking forward as a wing back and delivering a perfect cross which caused devastation in the Scarborough box.

Frank used his experience and hung back and waited to assess the bounce. You had to do this on the plastic as you didn't know if the ball was going rear up or skid through. He positioned himself perfectly, took one touch and smashed it low across the keeper into the far corner. This was the second goal created by an overlapping full back and it was such a dangerous asset to have as a team. An experienced centre forward knew how to take advantage and position themselves in the right areas. Frank set a record of scoring six goals in a League Cup match which still stands today. Sadly a few weeks later he was to sustain a knee injury from which he was not able to recover despite months and months of rehabilitation. This saddened everybody at the club as he was destined to miss the best part of his career.

We had shocked the football world in Britain at least with this devastating destruction of Scarborough and everyone waited for the visit of Arsenal in the next round to see how they would cope.

Amusing Anecdote 2: A funny incident regarding this game involves another family character who was like an uncle to me. He was my dad's best mate and was caretaker of Craven College, Skipton. His name is Barrie Howsen and he was a bit of a hard-man, but in a very nice way. He would finish stuff off but never started one! I had procured tickets for him, my father and Grandpa in the main stand at Oldham; in the same section were some Scarborough fans. They were boisterous and confident of success following the previous round defeat of Chelsea. One bloke in particular was sitting directly behind Barrie and was making derogatory comments about Oldham from the start of the game. As the demolition went on, instead of dampening down this bloke he just got more vitriolic. This was starting to piss Barrie right off because one comment was aimed at me, so when Frankie Bunn slammed in his sixth goal Barrie stood up and, in celebration, threw his elbows back behind him and caught the bloke square on the nose. He quickly left, blood dripping everywhere so, just like Scarborough, he received a bloody nose!

This match was to become one of those 'never-to-be-forgotten' games. Most fans remember particular games and will carry those memories to their graves; I am no different. I remember some of the games with agony and the others with ecstacy, and my lifetime has witnessed many such games. The first lasting memory for me came on the 27th January 1962 in a huge game at Boundary Park when the mighty Liverpool came to town for a fourth-round FA Cup tie. A massive 41,733 spectators were crushed into Boundary Park to watch Liverpool edge out the Latics by a score of 1-2. Liverpool took the lead in controversial fashion in the 73rd minute when Ian St John 'scored' with an in-off the bar goal reminiscent of Geoff Hurst's disputed 1966 World Cup final game. I was standing behind the goalmouth and could plainly see that St John's goal did not cross the line – oh for goal-line technology! Now I'm not one to hold a grudge, but I had to wait over 50 years until underdogs Athletic famously knocked Liverpool out of the FA Cup with an incredible 3-2 win at Boundary Park in 2013.

Boxing Day 1962 was another such memory when Southport were the visitors to a cold and snow covered Boundary Park; they went away with a stinging 11-0 defeat, Athletic's record score to this day and equalling their highest ever number of goals in one game. Bert Lister led the goal fest with six, Colin Whittaker scored a hat-trick, while John Colquhoun and Bob Ledger completed the rout. Athletic had led by 9 goals as early as the 53rd minute in a remarkable game. Master schemer Bobby Johnstone was the architect of the whole proceedings and was very unfortunate not to get on the score sheet himself. A crowd of 14,662 witnessed the demolition and I wondered if anyone would ever equal or beat Bert's six blast!

Wolverhampton Wanderers in the third-round of the FA Cup at Boundary Park on Saturday 28th January 1967 was another one of those 'never-to-be-forgotten' games. Manager Jimmy McIlroy had boldly blooded teenagers Ronnie Blair, Ian Wood and Les Chapman for the game and it seemed to have paid off as the Latics were two goals up after the regulation 90 minutes. Keith Bebbington got both goals in front of 24,968 enthusiastic supporters. Miraculously, Wolves got two goals in the dying minutes of added injury time to force a draw which left the

Latics' fans dumbfounded as they could not believe what had just happened before their very eyes; with hindsight, the ball should have been booted out of the stadium at every chance in those dying minutes – Wolves easily won the replay 4-1.

Leeds United visited Boundary Park on Sunday 17th May 1987 for the second leg of the Second Division promotion play-off games, the first year of such games. Leeds were a goal up from the first leg but Gary Williams soon put the teams level. Ex-Leeds players Andy Linighan, Tommy Wright and Denis Irwin all played against their old club while Andy Ritchie played for Leeds. Mike Cecere headed what looked like the winner just minutes from the end, but Leeds silenced the home fans when Edwards got his second last minute goal in two games. The 2-1 final scoreline for the Latics, watched by 19,216 supporters, meant that Leeds went through on the away goals rule. It was a bitter pill for the Boundary Park faithful to swallow, some of which were openly weeping at the end of the game. This was a 'never-to-be-forgotten game,' but for the wrong reasons. I still remember sitting in the car after the game with my mate for at least an hour analysing the game, too upset to even go for an after game pint. I now regard the terrible result as a turning point in the history of the club, as it was the catalyst for a new era in the fortunes of Oldham Athletic.

Back to the job in hand – the visit of Scarborough. The build up to the game was fantastic as they had just knocked out the mighty Chelsea over two legs in the last round. The Seadogs were obviously on a high and must have come into the game expecting a good result and hoping to build on their success, in addition to looking forward to a successful cup run.

'Big Joe' gave the following pre-match teaser, *'We have consistently 'blown it' when the cups have come around, never putting together a run, and whenever I speak to our supporters around the town, I am constantly reminded of this. There has been a feeling in the past that we desperately need to play big clubs with the accent on receiving a good revenue, whatever the result. Our financial position is still not what might be described as 'flushed with funds' but I can honestly say that a cup is second only in this season's priorities, with revenue a close third. Our overall objective is still promotion but the confidence and support we can gain from a cup run should not be underestimated. I am sure that there will be no shortage of atmosphere tonight, and with the presence of the TV cameras about us, we must make sure that the Latics are in the hat for the next round. Get behind the lads tonight, and let's make it a great week at Molineaux on Saturday.'* I had to read this over and over to fully comprehend just what Joe was saying. In hindsight, he must have had a crystal ball in his office with the way the season panned out and what was to happen in the subsequent seasons. I wonder if he could have forseen what was actually about to unfold, whether he might have changed his pre-match notes?

Little did Scarborough expect us to put them to the sword as quickly as we did. The Frankie Bunn goals in this game are very well documented but to actually be there to watch the demolition was something else. The first goal went in after 10 minutes and when Bunn completed his first-half hat-trick in the first twenty minutes the fans could feel that something special was going to happen that night. The cry of 'Frankie Bunn... Frankie Bunn... Frankie Bunn...' resonated around Boundary Park. To say that the excitement was electric would be an understatement.

Bunn rattled in his fourth goal in the 35th minute. He could have laid the ball off for Andy Ritchie to score but by this time he already had the scent for goals so he wasn't going to give it anybody else! By this time the fans had sensed that there was some kind of record to be broken on this special night but they were unsure of just what. The goals just kept going into the net and by half time it was 5-0 and all them had been scored by Frankie – it was becoming an astonishing night.

The second half began but, although Boro had done their best to reorganised themselves, the visitors only had one their minds and that was how to stop the onslaught which was facing them. Their task was like trying to make a sieve completely watertight with a thimbleful of salt! It didn't take long for the sixth goal to hit the net and what a cracker it was. Andy Ritchie hammered an unstoppable volley to claim the goal of the game, from all of 20 yards, but that man Bunn also took some of the credit as he had flicked the ball on for him. When Bunn volleyed in the seventh and final goal of the tie in the last minute of the game, I distinctly remember looking at the scoreboard which used to stand at the Rochdale Road end of the ground. Whoever was in charge of the board certainly had a sense of humour, and he worked his magic on that night as it distinctly flashed the score as ..... Bunn 6 Scarborough 0. Talk about rubbing it in! It was a new record for the League Cup as no other player had ever scored six goals in one match.

Another goal celebration with Stitch

In the after match interviews Bunn said that it hadn't sunk in yet as he hadn't realised that he was a record breaker. His previous best was two goals in a competitive match and three in a pre-season friendly. Rick Holden said it was his shot that the keeper fumbled and he had put it on a plate for Bunnie. Both Mike Milligan and Denis Irwin stated likewise and said it was their crosses and he coudn't miss them. Ritchie declared that he wasn't saying that Bunnie was greedy but he still had the bruises on both eye brows where Bunnie had knocked him away – I seemed to sense a little bit of banter in the statements.

One Latics' fan was in the RAF at the time and had travelled up from Huntingdon just to watch this game. He particularly remembers standing in the Chaddy End during the warm up as his mate Pete had just bought a couple of pies (as he usually did) and had already begun to devour his 'growlers.' Within a minute or so Neil Adams took a practice shot which sailed over the bar and smacked Pete straight in the chest smearing both of his meat and potato pies (which in those days were red-hot) all over him. It took Pete's mate about 20 minutes to stop laughing! Another supporter regards the Scarborough game as the start of some of the best football ever to be seen in the 'pinch me' era and it also made others sit up and take note of the Boundary Park boys.

Phil Taylor recalled, *"The Latics took an early lead when the keeper spilled one to Bunny who rolled it into an empty net. This fella in the Main Stand Paddock said, 'Ummm, it's the only way Bunn will score tonight!' I always found it amazing how Bunny split Latics fans' opinions so much, more than any other player I can recall. For me he was the catalyst in Oldham's greatest days. Anyhow, the wag started to shift uncomfortably around as Bunn scored numbers 2, 3, 4 and 5 all before half time and his scarf was over his face as the scoreboard announced Bunn 5 Boro 0. The second half was a bit of an anti-climax, Ritchie scored the best goal of the night and then Frank notched his sixth in the last minute. Six goals in one game, funny how the wag never openly mouthed criticism about Bunn ever again. It's a record that still stands today.... great memories."*

Everyone remembers the game for the usual record number of goals put away by Frankie Bunn – 6 goals – a record for the League Cup which will probably never be beaten but most agree that the best goal, no doubt, was Andy Richie's volley. Another regular was making his way home and, upon realising the coincidences, exclaimed, *"7 goals, 7,000 crowd, I'm going to drink 7 pints!"* which he convincingly did! As a result of all the aforementioned this game now drops comfortably into that 'never-to-be-forgotten' category.

Amusing Anecdote 3: The next day I was buzzing as I went to work. I was a grammar school teacher and was the only Oldham Athletic supporter among the staff. There was the usual band-waggon Manchester teams' supporters, a Leicester City supporter and a Burnley fan, along with a few local non-league followers. I worked in a separate block from the main school building which was in full view of all staff and students exiting the building. I made a huge sign from two sheets of A1 size paper – it was useful to be an Applied Engineering Graphics teacher – which simply read 7-0. It almost completely covered one of the large hallway windows in its entirety. I received several thumbs-up from the Oldham Athletic supporting students throughout the day but everyone else kept out of my way as they knew what a gloater I was.

Oldham v Arsenal – League Cup Fourth Round 1989/90 3-1

Wednesday 22nd November 1989
Boundary Park 7:30pm

OLDHAM		ARSENAL
Andy Rhodes	1	John Lucic
Dennis Irwin	2	Lee Dixon
Andy Barlow	3	Nigel Worthington
Nick Henry	4	Michael Thomas
Earl Barrett	5	David O'Leary
Paul Warhurst	6	Tony Adams
Ian Marshall	7	David Rocastle
Andy Ritchie	8	Kevin Richardson
Frank Bunn	9	Alan Smith
Mike Milligan	10	Niall Quinn
Rick Holden	11	Brian Marwood
Roger Palmer	12	Siggi Jonsson
Gary Williams	14	Perry Groves
Manager: Joe Royle		Manager: George Graham

Referee: RB Gifford (Llanbradach). Linesmen: JJ Shawcross (Northwich); R Shepherd (Guiseley).

Crowd: 14,932

This was the game of the round as far as the nation was concerned because every neutral wanted to see how the Champions, Arsenal, would get on against what was becoming every fan's second favourite team. Back in the day, 70s, 80s and early 90s, the League Cup in its various sponsor name guises was a very important competition and much coveted by the top teams. The creation of the Champions League and the influx of foreign managers made this less so and it wrongly became a less respected cup. However, Arsenal did not want to lose this.

The domestic treble of FA Cup, League Cup and First Division was the stuff of legends and the crowd size on the night at Boundary Park certainly bore this out! The attendance for the Scarborough game was 7,713, but tonight's game practically doubled this with 14,924. We were nearing full capacity in a matter of months but this showed the excitement of the cup competitions as the league gates were still only 7,000 to 8,000 which was a little bit of a disappointment. Throughout the whole league season of 1989/90 only Oxford United had a lower average attendance than us at the Latics with 5,000 as opposed to our 6,500!

If you look at the Arsenal line up they were all 'big names' household names, with lots of Internationals spread throughout the team. Joe was, as were the whole of Oldham Athletic's programme writers, very respectful to Arsenal Football Club and rightly so – they were top of the league and, as mentioned, current champions of English football. Like the Scarborough encounter, I was the only player on our team to have recent experience of playing against Arsenal. I had played against them in February 1988 for Watford in a First Division match at Highbury and I scored the only goal in a 1-0 victory. I knew the way they played, which was very direct and, although some players had moved on, they were essentially the same outfit. They had obviously improved to win the league but I went to spy on them on the Tuesday evening and also watched them train and I immediately picked up on something.

They had obviously come a day earlier to try to familiarise themselves with our plastic pitch which was getting a reputation as big as the team, but no really big side had come a cropper on it yet. Leeds did but there weren't any complaints from them because they had lost at home also and they had played on it several times before. As commented, Arsenal were direct and only played football in the final third, but they got the ball into the final third usually by way of a long ball to Alan Smith or Niall Quinn. They were both very tall had good close control and were good headers of the ball. What they weren't blessed with was pace and so our back four were not going to get run ragged that was for sure. They solved this soon after by signing Ian Wright from Crystal Palace, he could get on the end of the flick-ons and then it was 'bang' straight in the back of the net.

Earl Barrett was quick and elastic and very difficult to get past. He stuck to players like glue. Paul Warhurst was simply the fastest footballer in England at the time and no player had a hope in hell of getting in behind him. Arsenal had tall players, Quinny, Smith, David O'Leary and Tony Adams who were in short, not suited to this type of surface. On this surface you needed a low centre of gravity and the ability to change direction very quickly as the slightest change in angle caused these big guys problems.

When I watched The Arsenal train I was surprised in what I saw. I was renting a minging small flat above Garforth Glass in Lees and had time on my hands, so I went down and spied on them from the stands. No doubt I was clocked but what could they do? They just played five-a-side tip tap football. George Graham set up his pattern of play and went through his gambits at a very pedestrian pace. They didn't hit any long balls at all. I got the feeling that they had decided that you couldn't play long balls on the plastic. And they didn't!

The game began. They kicked off and kept the ball for five minutes but we just sat in and let them have it. Then we pressed and took it off them and played a long ball diagonally over their back four which I saw and instantly bamboozled them. I will never forget the look on Tony Adam's face when this happened and they suddenly knew they were in for a game. We pegged Arsenal back and should have been in the lead long before we eventually were, right on the stroke of half time. Joe had played an unusual line up by leaving out Roger Palmer and Neil Adams and playing three strikers up front in Ian Marshall, Frankie Bunn and Andy Ritchie.

Andy played more on the right as a winger which he had done at Leeds United and cleverly knew the role very well combining of a winger and a centre forward at the same time. He gave Nigel Winterburn all sorts of positional dilemmas because of his movement and it was this movement that set him up to score the first goal. Andy Barlow played a beautiful diagonal ball over the Arsenal back four into the area and Winterburn wasn't anywhere to be seen. Andy chested it down and hammered a volley which seemed to cut my old mate John Lukic in half. The crowd went mad.

Arsenal had obviously had the Gaffer in their ear at half time and we knew this would be the case. We used to listen to their half time team talks by standing up against the adjoining door which led from the home shower and bath area into theirs. Of course we always locked it on match days and of course they didn't know we had people standing the other side listening to every word. Joe and Willy warned us of the obvious fact that Arsenal would come out and have a go at the start of the second half which is just what they did. We knew that we had to weather the storm which, thanks to Andy Rhodes making three crucial saves, we did. Andy was a spectacular shot stopper and had marvellous athleticism. A header from Niall Quinn was destined for the top corner but Rhodesy lept like a salmon and hoiked it out of the goal. Brilliant save and that inspired us to get the job done.

In the 64th minute Mike Milligan (Sean O'Hooligan as I called him) made a break and was upended by David O'Leary on the edge of the box which brought him a booking. The Arsenal back four were now earning that famous phrase we conjured up for visiting defenders to Boundary Park – 'dogs on lino' and it was obvious they clearly couldn't cope with our high tempo passing and movement. I fancied a go at the free kick but chose to smash it rather than curl or place it and it smashed straight into the wall. Fortunately the ball bounced to Nick Henry at the edge of the box who half volleyed it straight passed Lukic. He had a good strike on him had Nick, but he had not managed to realise his goal scoring as much as his good technique should have allowed him. He regularly spanked shots in like that in training and it was no surprise to me when he killed Arsenal like this.

We piled on more pressure and ten minutes later we scored again with Andy grabbing his second. This was a real forward's master class in passing and moving and should be shown to aspiring young strikers. Andy had come in off the wing and had enough awareness to turn and run. Denis Irwin saw the opportunity to bomb forward and Andy released him. The Arsenal back four were so deep by now it was untrue and, as Andy carried on his run, nobody picked him up and he headed in point blank from the six yard box – game over!

The Arsenal fans were silent and the Arsenal players stunned. They were well beaten and we even missed more easy chances to make the score five or six which wouldn't have flattered us. At the end big Niall Quinn somehow looped his foot around the ball and it went into the top corner. Rhodesy almost had it but it didn't matter, only from the point of view that it was a little disappointing that we hadn't kept a clean sheet, but we were there and into the quarter finals. The mood in the dressing room was electric and I guess around the town also. The town was set to get cup fever for the next six months and it was a marvellous feeling to start to prove ourselves and to become the talk of the national press also.

After the game we were all invited to Norman Leisure which was a club owned by Norman Holden, my namesake but no immediate relation, who was a director at the club (incidentally, only a Lancastrian could name a company 'Norman Leisure'). Joe had some business interest in it too but I don't know the details. We had a couple of drinks and then went home because we had a game on the Saturday away to Ipswich. We were still to really get going in the league which Joe insisted was his priority. Personally it was my eighteenth consecutive game of the season and I was improving as a player all the time. Consistency of selection helped my confidence and my fitness and I didn't think anyone could stop me doing what I wanted to do on a football pitch, and I was very contented. I knew we were going places.

Amusing Anecdote 4: My dad kicked Andy Ritchie's pint over at the club which was funny, because Andy wouldn't let him buy him another one and we all raised an eyebrow at this! Andy visits often to the Isle of Man and we play golf and have a few beers and a reminisce and my dad always tries to repay him he never allows him to do so!

This was one massive game for the fans. The First Division Champions were coming to little Oldham. Boundary Park was rocking and the Chaddy End was full to capacity. Woe betide anyone who had 'tanked-up' before the game as there would be no way of getting to the toilets in a rush, as everyone was shoulder to shoulder. I have actually witnessed fans urinating in the Chaddy End before! It was obvious to everyone when a semi-circle slowly opened up in front of the perpetrator and the people in front would turn round and give extremely dirty looks to him; he usually had a relieved, smiling face by this time. This could not possibly happen against Arsenal as there was no room to move foreward. If it was to happen I would expect that several people would be going home with warm, wet legs and would also expect one person to be going home with a swollen lip or a bursted nose!

Joe Royle admitted in his programme notes that he would have liked to have gone into the game with a victory under his belt instead of the 1-1 home draw with Brighton & Hove Albion, although he confessed that it was a match that could have been lost only 12 months ago. He also realised the enormity of the task of taking on the Gunners. He concluded with the hope of a good game and the fall of a very formidable 'red wall.'

Athletic entered the match knowing that it was 22 games and 11 months since they had last lost at Boundary Park but, to add spice, they were playing the Gunners who had been League Cup finalists in two out of the last three seasons. The match got under way with the Latics playing towards the Chaddy End and every slip, mis-pass, off-target shot and lost ball by the visitors was cheered and jeered by the joyous home fans who could sense something dramatic was going to happen. Just before the half time whistle, a lovely centre from local lad Andy Barlow was struck home by that man again – Andy Ritchie. This was becoming a trait but a damned good one! The home fans, including myself, suddenly got the feeling that we were never going to lose this game and the cry of 'Here we go... Here we go... Here we go...' reverberated around the ground. In fact, the way we were now playing, we might not lose another match this season, cup or league! Such was the relentless cavalier approach and the unmittigating, dogged determination of the team that the fans felt fully justifed in their high expectations.

The champions were forced to spring into action in the second half but Michael Thomas, Lee Dixon and Niall Quinn were all thwarted by excellent saves from Andy Rhodes between the Athletic sticks who was playing out of his skin. The pendulum swung back in Athletic's favour when 20-year-old Nick Henry notched his first ever Latics goal with a fantastic 23 yard volley. It came after Mike Milligan was taken down on the edge of the box by David O'Leary who was yellow carded; there was no 'professional foul' or automatic red cards in those days. Ritchie popped up again to head home an insurance goal, his eighth goal in the last nine matches, to make it 3-1. Ritchie's second goal was the cue for the Oldham fans to burst into the chant of, 'We want seven,' in memory of the Bunn-fest against Scarborough. Arsenal had to be contented with a late consolation goal from Quinn. This was greeted almost by silence as by then the damage was well and truly done and the home side were through to the quarter-finals for the first time in their history!

Any such thoughts that it was all down to the plastic surface was unmerited, with many visiting teams using the cynical approach by using it as an excuse for being outplayed. In fact, it was more difficult for the Oldham players as they had to adapt week after week from grass to plastic – what kind of an advantage is that? George Graham described the pitch as 'no excuse' and after the match he graciously confessed, *"I was very disappointed with my team's performance. Giantkilling is usually about desperate, scruffy victories yet Oldham took on their superiors and battered them. They were everything a power team should be: exceptionally fit and direct in the best sense of the word, mixing urgent interplay with a stream of early crosses."* Praise indeed!

'Fryatt' summed up the night as, *"Fantastic night – the ground was rocking – beat Arsenal in every department. Three great goals. Ritchie gave Tony Adams, the England centre-half, a torrid time. The Chaddy End was shut at 7:15pm, such was the crush."*

Another fan declared, *"If there was ever a defining moment when Athletic became stamped on the public consciousness, it was when Andy Ritchie slammed in the first in the League Cup game versus Arsenal. I was half way up the Chaddy End, behind the nets, and the explosion of joy was more than a goal celebration – it was the lifetime of pain associated with supporting Oldham being exorcised from 15,000 souls in one split-second. Although something special had been bubbling and brewing for a year or two, this was the second when we KNEW we weren't just good, but a match for any team in the land. From that day on, newspapers couldn't print enough back page photographs of Ritchie wheeling away from goal, arm outstretched in salute. The good thing was that Latics fans could proudly talk about their team's exploits the world over. On the other hand, the Arsenal fans making their way up Sheepfoot Lane after the match were overheard conspiring to keep secret, on returning to the capital, their presence at Boundary Park on the occasion of such a comprehensive and humiliating drubbing... "*

Memories from Phil Taylor, *"This was the game when I finally thought 'Oldham have arrived!' I had been watching Latics since 1970 and our cup hadn't exactly been overflowing with success, particularly the League Cup where we had been to the third round once before, only to get thrashed at Fulham. Arsenal was our biggest home cup tie since a third round home FA cup match with Spurs but we would be in the quarter-finals if we could overcome the Gunners. I was more than a little bit nervous as, although I was enjoying football at Latics more than anytime in 15 years, we hadn't beaten a top division side in any cup since the 1920s.... I needn't have worried as Latics were magnificent. The Gunners backline couldn't cope with the imperious Frank Bunn who led the line brilliantly. Nick Henry scored the opener from about 80 yards (or so it seemed...) and hysteria hit the famous Oldham ground.... Latics were beating the Arsenal."*

"Andy Ritchie, what a player he was; best £50,000 we had ever spent – thanks Billy Bremner – He weighed in with two more goals and we were humiliating the famous Arsenal. Their front pairing of Niall Quinn and Alan Smith (both about 8ft 6 ins) only defeated the superb Barrett and Warhurst in the last minute to give them a totally flattering scoreline of Oldham 3 Arsenal 1. The match attracted a crowd just shy of 15,000 to Boundary Park and the country was being treated to the emergence of a wonderfully entertaining little football club who were to grace the nation for a short period. I couldn't believe my eyes, my beautiful little Latics had hammered mighty Arsenal and were in the quarter-final draw. I went back to my girlfriend's that night and her dad (lovely bloke but not easily impressed by sporting icons) waxed lyrical about how wonderful the Latics had been, and what a performance Bunny had put in against the Arsenal back four. Glory days were here for the Latics faithful. I just hope we see their like again."

Amusing Anecdote 5: A young fan remembers the game as the time that 'legend' Andy Ritchie knocked him on his backside in the pre-match warm up after a 25-yard-screamer missed the target and smashed him in his face. He said that Andy must have felt guilty as he decided to keep his shots on target in the match. That fan was only nine at the time but by then his blood ran royal blue and he distinctly remembers the ironic cheers when Arsenal got their consilation goal.

Oldham v Everton – FA Cup Fifth Round Trilogy 1989/90 2-2; 1-1; 2-1.

Saturday 17th February 1990
Boundary Park 7:30pm

OLDHAM		EVERTON
Jon Hallworth	1	Neville Southall
Dennis Irwin	2	Ian Snodin
Andy Barlow	3	Neil McDonald
Nick Henry	4	Kevin Ratcliffe
Ian Marshall	5	David Watson
Earl Barratt	6	Norman Whiteside
Neil Adams	7	John Ebbrell
Andy Ritchie	8	Stuart McCall
Roger Palmer	9	Graeme Sharp
Mike Milligan	10	Tony Cottee
Rick Holden	11	Kevin Sheedy
Neil Redfearn	12	Mike Newell
Paul Warhurst	14	Martin Keown
Manager: Joe Royle		Manager: Colin Harvey

Referee: AW Ward (London). Linesmen: T Lynch (Middlesbrough); GH Lyner (Gainsborough).

Crowd: 19,320

This game came straight after the mid-week 6-0 demolition of West Ham in the semi-final of the League Cup. We were on a high but were also physically tired, simply because we had put everything into that semi-final first leg. It is for this reason that I believe we were behind so early on and the fact that Everton came out of the traps 'on fire' and determined to finish us off quickly. They nearly did. If they had score a third before half time we would have gone under. The overriding impression I got from Everton was one of aggression, and not just 'contact sport aggression,' but one of intimidation and bullying both of us as a team and of the officials.

They had four players booked by 60 minutes and our first goal: Kevin Sheedy; Neil McDonald; Graeme Sharp and Stuart McCall. I knew what this lot were like as I had played against them in my First Division debut for Watford in 1988 and was shocked at how aggressive as a unit they were – very physical and strong and always at the referee and linemen. Their side had developed since then but not necessarily in a skilled way. When I played against them in March 1988 the two opponents I was up against was the England pairing of Gary Stevens at right back and Trevor Steven at right wing. Now I say 'two' because often I was doubled up against by the full back and the winger and I had to learn how to cope with this. This pair was a class act and it was difficult to make an impression against them. The current incumbents were not in the same league, Snodin and Ebbrell, although Snodin in my opinion was a very fine footballer who was probably better suited to midfield than right back. Funnily enough both Steven and Stevens had cleared off across the border to play for Glasgow Rangers, leaving a considerable hole to fill on the right.

Everton had come out flying, and the defence had stood up magnificently to stop them mauling us. Jon Hallworth, back from injury, made a magnificent save when we were two nil down and if they had scored then it would have been the end of the tie. Everton did score early though through Sharp in the 22nd minute after we had put them under some early pressure, from which we should have scored at least one goal. Neil Adams had a volley blocked by Sheedy and they cleared a header from Marshy off the line. But it was a mistake from Earl that led to Sharp's goal; he was prone to them occasionally but aren't all defenders? Earl's attributes were tremendous athleticism and elasticity in the tackle (I also have that in my tackle!), but I used to accuse him of having his boots on the wrong feet at times when it came to passing the ball. He gave me stick for being a Wur and I gave him stick for passing the ball.

As a centre half the one skill Earl didn't have, that say Marshy had, was the ability to hit me with a 60 yard diagonal from the edge of our area. When he played left back at Barnsley once, every pass intended for me either went over my head into the stand or was cut out by their right winger. At half time Joe gave me a bollocking for not being involved in the game, calling me a passenger, yet it was Earl's fault but Joe never used to bollock him! It drove me nuts but I couldn't protest my innocence because that was 'grassing someone up,' so I just bollocked Earl myself. Still it was unfortunate (but not unexpected) that his 'fly-hack' was volleyed superbly by Sharp and, although Hallworth got a hand to the ball, it flew into the top corner. My heart sank, I thought that perhaps our time was running out. It was compounded four minutes or so later when Tony Cottee pounced on another defensive mistake and made it two nil. I just couldn't believe it!

One thing changed though after that goal. The Everton players ran towards their fans in the Rochdale Road end, and as Ian Snodin ran past Milly he deliberately smashed him in the back with his shoulder. I thought, 'right you bastard, you are having it!' The next fifty-fifty challenge I just went barging straight over him and dumped him on the floor. I had had enough of their intimidation and it was now time to start meting out a bit of their own medicine.

In the dressing room at half time we were quite animated and incensed about what had happened and about Everton's approach. I was all for smashing them physically but the gaffer just told us to keep playing and that we would get our rewards, justice if it existed, would come. Sure enough a piece of luck occurred when Neville Southall took out Roger Palmer and we got a penalty. They of course protested the event and surrounded the referee, trying to do a Franz Beckenbaur and make him change his mind like he did for Bayern Munich against Leeds in the 1975 European Cup Final, but Mr Ward was having none of it and I think that he was pretty sick of them by now as he booked McCall for his dissent.

Andy Ritchie was coolness personified, like he always was, and duly smashed home the penalty sending 'Big Nev' the wrong way. We were back in business. I sensed fear in the Everton side because of our relentless attacking approach but they were still dangerous in attack themselves. For that reason the gaffer took Neil Adams off as early as the 30th minute to try to shore up the defence with Paul Warhurst's pace. Equally, that allowed us more attacking power by pushing Marshy up front which allowed Roger to play on the right but more as a centre forward who would sniff out goals. I felt sorry for Bert (Neil Adams) but needs must and the big man, Joe, was proved right when we scored our equalizer.

The anatomy of the equalizer was quite simple in that it was a deep cross from me to the far post and Roger headed home, but the philosophy of its construction was well rehearsed in training. The Rochdale Road end was an open terrace, not like it is now, and the wind used to hold the ball up and make it hang when I crossed it from deep. I had noticed this and therefore often used to stand the ball up as high as I could to confuse the defence and the keeper. They found it difficult to attack the ball because it used to slow down as it reached the area and allow our forwards who knew this (especially Rodge) to attack the ball late. This is what happened.

Nobody closed me down. I suspected that they were tired, so I put in a big looping cross which Roger read and headed home. Southall hesitated and this, in goalkeeping terms, was fatal and it was 2-2. I have read some of the reports, written by Bob Young of the *Oldham Chronicle*, and he can never make his mind up about me. I was sometimes called mercurial and on other occasions he used to find adjectives to describe me like 'loping' and 'plodding' but he didn't know what we knew about the wind and crosses from that area of the pitch, and neither did Neville Southall. He looked bemused as Roger got to it first but it wasn't Neville's fault, he had just been done, that's all. The match finished 2-2 and that evening I can remember being too tired to go out so I went home early. Normally we would have a couple of beers and a meal but I was drained. It had been a long week and now we faced a replay at Goodison Park and we were falling behind in the league.

The crowd at Boundary Park was capacity for the second time in a week, and the first time we had sell-outs for years. The Oldham faithful certainly made themselves heard – it was a tremendous atmosphere and I wondered where all the fans had come from! We had had a huge crowd of 18,000 in the replay of the League Cup quarter-final against Southampton but this was the first week in years that the ground was full. Incidentally, in the ensuing couple of years or so, the ground was bursting at the seams and it used to tickle us when Hillary read out the gate size over the tannoy to announce that 'today's attendance is 14,323' or some other such low figure. We would look around and see the place starining at the edges and we knew Mr Hardy's little scheme for the tax man! Whoops, I can't say that can I? Well I just have and what are the Inland Revenue going to do about it now anyway?

First Replay:
We then had to go over to Liverpool for the replay which was a distraction we could have done without, because I agreed with the gaffer that what we wanted was promotion and to be visiting places like this on a regular bread and butter basis – after all we had proved we were good enough against top class opposition anyway, so what was the problem? The problem was we were in the Second Division and wasting our time against promotion in blasted cup runs! The fans of course loved it, as did the media and the hierarchy of Oldham Athletic. I had fortunately tasted the First Division before and so did several other players but the feeling amongst the boys was, 'great as it was, it was not realistic!'

During the replay, things got worse on the intimidation front as Everton tried to bully us on their own patch. Again the back four were superb but, more than anyone, our midfield duo of Mick Milligan and Nick Henry were absolutely awesome. They made my life so easy it was untrue. They closed people down like throwing a blanket over the opposition. Managers like Graham Taylor were later to compliment Oldham for our pressing skills 'high up the pitch' rather like Barcelona do today, but it was Milly and Nick that he was referring to. They were all over Everton and everyone else in this 'Golden Period' like a bad rash, and so much so that it drove Norman Whiteside to the edge of his wits culminating in him being sent off in the replay for a nasty foul on Milly. Everton, to their shame, had five more players booked in addition to that sending off!

Marshy had a goal disallowed for being too strong on Neville Southall, which I think the Keepers Union would remain quiet about (he went down like a Fred Dibnah chimney) and then he scored a good header from a cross that I again stood up, which I knew Nev didn't like. They then got a dubious penalty which Kevin Sheedy put away. It was his only real contribution of the game such was Dennis Irwin's mastery of him. So, after extra time, it was back to Boundary Park for another replay! Christ!

Second Replay:
I will never forget this game in life and death as I intend to remember it forever. We had them back at our patch and I, for one, was determined to see these f**kers off! Everton to their credit were less aggressive and came out of the traps flying again to take an early lead in the 12th minute. The gaffer had changed things around and gone for three at the back which, well, I was happy with. It meant that I had the two raptors, Milly and Nick, inside me, and my great friend Neil Redfearn, the best two-footed midfielder in the country and best passer of a ball, on the pitch at the same time. Their goal was a result of the three at the back situation but the ultimate win was as a result of Joe's daring to overload the attack with two wingers, me and Bert, two forwards, Marshy and Rodge, and three midfielders as mentioned. We steam rolled them but couldn't finish them off!

At one nil down, it was the first time that I didn't panic because I knew that we would win but we still had work to do! Then Neil McDonald – who I didn't like at the time because of his arrogance when I played for Watford, and scored the winner, the previous year in an equally enthralling FA Cup second replay scenario against Newcastle – passed a dodgy ball back to 'Big Nev' and Roger Palmer pounced. In the Newcastle trilogy, Neil had asked me how many England caps I had won and I just told him none because I wasn't good enough. I also told him that he was only in the set up because he was an 'arse licker,' which didn't go down well.

Anyway Roger being Rodge, wrote Southall off in true 'OOOooooh Roger Palmer' style. He was christened by Joe as 'The Black Assassin' but you can't say that today can you, as you might get an eight game ban like Luis Suarez? Rodge apart from being the top goal scorer of all time at Athletic, despite not being able to kick a ball properly at times, was also the most fearless striker we had and he took no prisoners! He went for the fifty-fifty with Nev and saw him off, and the ball went into the back of the net! It was like a meerkat against a rhino but the meerkat won. 'The Assassin' had struck again; they withered but saw it through to extra time!

"I know what you have been up to - pull your finger out or you're for it!"

I knew we had to win and that is what we did in true legend style with Marshy scoring the winning penalty. It went like this; Marshy scourged into the area like a dead man walking but full of hell because he wanted to put one over on his old club who, he had always told me, had let him down as they thought him lazy! Ian Marshall comes into the category of best players never to play for England and, in my opinion, he is a better player than Arsenal's Tony Adams will ever be. He was desperate to prove all the scousers wrong and he did. He was up-ended by my old sparring partner, Neil McDonald – it couldn't have been anyone better – and then he picked himself up to score the penalty to Southall's right. He struck it like a thunderbolt and Marshy could hit a ball!

Marshy then did something that would get him locked up today. He ran towards the Everton fans in the Rochdale Road End and outstretched his arms and extended two fingers on each hand and 'veed-off' the whole of their contingent. Scandalous, hilarious and deserved! His father did receive a brick through his front window for Marshy's actions, however. I think he upset them somewhat. He, more than anyone, deserved this win and it sent shock waves through the country! Oldham Athletic was now the best team in the land and Joe Royle had created a monster! It would get better!

Joe Royle told an amusing story following this trilogy. The Everton directors and chairman were in the Boundary Park boardroom after the game drowning their sorrows and having a bite to eat. The president of Oldham Athletic, Mr Schofield, said to them, *"never mind lads, at least you made a few bob!"* Absolute classic role reversal stuff.

Amusing Anecdote 6: During the extra time break there is a famous picture of Joe with his hand around my jaw and it was always portrayed as him smiling and encouraging me on to 'endeavour to persevere' in a genial 'matey' point of view! Nothing could be further from the truth. He was bollocking me because he knew that we had been out on the Thursday after the West Ham game and he said to me, *'You had better win this game or you are up for the high jump,'* or words to that effect! Why he always picked on me is anyone's guess!

This was a Colin Harvey v Joe Royle game. The ex-teammates who had played together in an FA Cup Final now had to face each other in a battle of wits. The Toffees had previously played in eleven FA Cup Finals, winning four of them while the Latics had only ever reached the semi-finals on two occasions. Everton came to Boundary Park to face a team which had been on such a run that they forgot what it was like to lose a game as they had lost just two of their last sixteen games. A frenzy had built up and the belief that Royle's army could not be beaten was prominent in both the Oldham fans as well as the players. The run at Boundary Park was phenominal and statisticians would have to rake back for over a year to find the last home defeat. The bookies didn't know where to go as the form book was being constantly over-turned and, yet again, Second Division Latics entered the game as favourites. The home side were challenging for promotion and, barring a miracle, had a Wembley visit in their sights for the final of the League Cup. To make the game even more exciting, Everton came as last season's cup finalists.

Game One:

The same team that thrashed West Ham 6-0 took to the Boundary Park artificial turf field with Neil Redfearn and Paul Warhurst making up the numbers on the bench. As a matter of interest, the average age of the home team was just 24. Everton came with the fillip that they were one of the last teams to win at Boundary Park, albeit it was a long time ago as the Latics had clocked-up 32 home games without defeat. Tony Cottee was the player who got both goals in the last visit and he was understandably in the starting line up for the Toffees. The game got off at a dramatic pace which almost resulted in disaster for the visitors. A long through ball from Ian Marshall was headed on and a back-pass from Snodin was fumbled by Everton keeper Neville Southall but his blushes were spared when McDonald kicked the ball away to safety. A great ball from Ritchie to Adams sent him off on a run which resulted in a corner, and a caution for Neil McDonald. Captain Sheedy complained too severely to the referee and he was also cautioned so two of the visitors were booked in the space of one minute, both apparently for dissent. The crowd loved it!

The game was evenly balanced with plenty of action in both boxes. Everton scored in the 22nd minute after Earl Barrett missed a low cross and Graeme Sharp was on hand to give the visitors the lead. A desperate effort by Latics' keeper Hallworth, who got a hand to it, just wasn't enough to keep the ball out. Barrett would be having nightmares for some time about his mistake. Sharp headed on a long through ball and he was tackled from the back by Marshall, which should have brought a penalty, but Cottee was 'Johnny-on-the-spot' to put the ball home and give Everton a 2-0 lead. Warhurst was brought on to replace Neil Adams. Hallworth was called upon again to prevent Cottee from making it 3-0 for the Toffees when he caught the ball with a really good save when it looked an easier option to tip round for a corner. A struggle was on at 2-0 but 3-0 could have been insurmountable. It was all Everton and they had their tails up. In a rare break, Irwin put Marshall away who slotted past Southall but the referee brought the game back for an off-side – it was a very close call and the half-time whistle blew with the score at 2-0 and Athletic trudged off very wet and very unhappy with things.

The second half kicked off with Oldham being the only team left in both major cups. Was it to last? Marshall was brought down by McCall some 30 yards out – well within striking range for someone with Denis Irwin's ability, and that's just what he did. The ball hit the wall, Warhurst chipped it forwards and Palmer raced with Southall for the ball and Southall dropped it, but Palmer was penalised for a foul. Minutes later Marshall headed the ball forwards once again and Palmer again set off in a race for possession and there was a mad scramble between three players which resulted in Southall lunging his leg which Palmer fell over. Southall ended up being launched like an acrobat in the circus but at the end of this melee the referee decided that the keeper had fouled Palmer and pointed to the spot to award a penalty, much to the delight of the home fans. Everton protested most vehemently. Andy Ritchie stepped up and calmly planted the ball into the bottom left of the net much to the chagrin of Southall. A bemused keeper picked the ball out of the net and kicked the ball away in disgust. With 30 minutes left, could Athletic salvage anything from the game?

Another move began when Ritchie did a neat turn and the ball went through for Palmer who blasted the ball goalwards but a great save by Southall brought a sign of relief from the now nail-biting Evertonians. Oldham started to pressure the visitors and the visiting keeper deprived Marshall of a goal with another addition to his string of saves. With time running out Everton began the possession game and tried to run the clock down. In the 67th minute Holden received the ball in his own half and set off for the dead ball line before whipping a centre over which was met perfectly by Palmer who headed the ball downwards past the hapless Southall for the equaliser. It was sheer textbook. The home crowd went wild! The goal was Palmer's 10th of the season and his 130th all-time goal. Although Palmer took all the accolades you would not see a better cross come over than that dispatched by Holden, it just invited a goal.

A flick-on from Sharp was chested down by Whiteside and Cottee got the ball in the net again but the whistle had already gone for pushing. Henry was the next player to put the ball in the net, just seconds later, but this one was disallowed for off-side. What a game it was turning out to be. Ritchie sent the ball over and Marshall headed it down to Palmer who ghosted in at the near post but Southall pulled out all the stops yet again to prevent a winner by pressuring Palmer into an early shot which went for a dead ball. Ritchie was next in line to test the keeper with a hard shot to the left but he responded with a fine one handed save. The last few seconds of play saw Marshall take a run on the left but Southall sprinted out of his area to blast the ball to safety. The game had been a quality cup tie with both sides giving everything and fighting for everything. No-one could dispute that Royle's youngsters had done well to fight back and that they fully deserved another bite of the cherry. The last thing Oldham wanted was a replay but a trip to Goodison Park was now on the agenda. Both sets of players left the field with their arms around the opposition and, for the fans at least, the waggon continued to roll on. Next episode on Wednesday.

First Replay:

Both teams made changes from the previous match but Oldham had to suffer a major blow when 25 goal Andy Ritchie aggravated a thigh strain and had to drop out. He was replaced up front by ex-Evertonian Ian Marshall who was one of the most versatile players around as he was equally at home in defence or leading the attack. Marshall declared that he only ever remember scoring one goal for Everton but the records have him down as having scored twice. It was the little stint up front by Marshall that had inspired the fight-back by Oldham in the previous game. Ray Atteveld was brought in to replace John Ebbrell for Everton. Everton were on a great run of home form and had only lost two of their games in the 1989/90 season. In comparison, Oldham had only won 4 of their 18 away games so Everton looked to start as favourites.

Oldham, playing in red, had an early chance with a through ball which both Palmer and Holden, despite their efforts, could not catch and the ball went dead. Sheedy was put through but, when it looked easier to score, he scuffed the ball over the bar from very close range with only Hallworth to beat. Whiteside took an early booking in the 18th minute – his eighth of the season. The Latics had lots of early pressure although not many goalworthy efforts were seen. A long range shot by Andy Barlow bounced wickedly in front of Southall but he managed to scramble it away for a corner. Royle''s record buy at £165,000 from Watford, Rick Holden, was brought down and the resultant free kick was taken by Barlow. The ball went straight into the net but for some unknown reason the referee penalised Ian Marshll to cancel out the strike. Upon reflection the striker had jumped with a high elbow so it could have been construed as dangerous play. At the end of the first half Holden had centred the ball but Marshall and Kevin Ratcliffe ended up in a skirmish which brought a whistle for a free kick, but it was the last action of the half and both teams left the field with the score at 0-0.

With Oldham already destined for a 60 game season, it was quite conceivable that this game could also go to another replay. They started the second half putting pressure on the home side by being quicker to the ball and there was no distinction between the two sides. A casual observer would not have known which team was the First Division side. Three minutes into the half, a tackle from Whiteside on Milligan instigated a lot of pushing and shoving which occurred right outside the Oldham dugout. Sharp was shouting at Milligan who was destitute on the floor and the resultant action from the referee witnessed Whiteside being sent off. This brought jubilation to the Oldham faithful as he was not a popular player due to his previous connection with the enemy down at Old Trafford. The game had taken a turn and was getting nasty. As for team spirit, Oldham exhibited a generosity of it. When Everton tried to boot them off the pitch they did not respond in kind. Sharp continued to intervene and his persistence saw him receive a yellow card! Both sets of crowds were booing for their different reasons but it needed to calm down – if only *Worzel Gummidge* could have entered the field with a set of calm heads for all the players!

When normal play resumed Barlow gave away a free kick in a dangerous position which kept Hallworth dancing around on his line while the wall was being set up. Sheedy hit the ball through the wall but the keeper beat the ball away to safety. With two minutes remaining Cottee went on another run, he was brought down and won a free kick. Sheedy hit the post from the resultant kick and the ball bounced out and it was Sheedy again in the last minute in a one-on-one with Hallworth but the stopper knocked the ball away yet again. After three-and-a half minutes of injury time the referee brought the game to an end with the score still 0-0. This meant another 30 minutes of torture for both sets of fans as well as taxing the fitness of both sets of players.

In the first period of extra time another impressive run by Holden resulted in a delicately floated centre from that deft left foot directly onto the head of Marshall who couldn't really miss as centres don't come any better that that. Marshall celebrated the goal not with the integrity of todays players facing their old team, but he relished the fact that he had scored over his old employers. Sharp had a chance to redress the balance minutes later but he could only send the ball over the bar with only Hallworth to beat. Sharp then won a penalty after Hallworth was judged to have caught him after he had chipped the ball over; ironically the ball clipped the top of the bar and went to safety. With six minutes remaining, Sheedy scored the penalty which brought a huge sigh of relief over Goodison after he had rifled the shot home. The ten men of Everton had fought back to earn a second replay.

Sheedy later admitted that he didn't think it was a penalty but he also thought that justice had been done due to the penalty that was given against them at Boundary Park. Marshall confessed after the game that the amount of fixtures the club had played was really taking its toll on the players. He had left the field with a dead-leg which needed treatment. When asked which role he preferred he admitted that after that match he would rather play up front than in defence. He reckoned that the opposition have trouble marking him because of his 'lollopy' stride but he also added that he didn't like being switched about all the time.

One fan said that his biggest memory of the whole encounter was the guy on the PA system at the end of the game. He announced, "The second replay will be staged at ...." there was total silence from a crowd of 35,000 .... it must have lasted a good ten seconds .... then he uttered .... Boundary Park." One of the Latics' board members had just won the toss in the board room and 4,000 travelling Latics fans just exploded. It was a great end to the game and Norman Whiteside had been sent off too!

Amusing Anecdote 7: On a personal note this game was on my mind for days. I was acting in a school drama production and we had a full rehearsal before the game. How long was this going to last and would I be in time for the game? I had a word with the director and told him of my predicament. I didn't want to let him down but priorities had to be met. There was no way I was going to miss the replay. I don't know how long the rehearsal dragged on but I do know that my car must have been burning rubber that night. As soon as I had finished my part, and got the nod from the director, there was no holding me. It was such a long time ago that I don't remember the specifics of the time but I must have had an hour to get to Goodison Park. I do remember having to park near the ground and the obligatory two kids came up with the usual, *"Watch your car for you mister?"* I was so desperate to get into the ground that I agreed to pay them a deposit up front with more to come after the game. I don't usually park near the ground but on that night it was a case of 'needs must.' I don't remember if the kids were still up after the extra time but all was well with my car so I got out of that one all right.

Second Replay: Before this match kicked off, Latics' boss Joe Royle received his 'manager of the month' award for February. The first two episodes of this encounter had produced lots of ill feeling between these competitive teams and 'Chapter Three' was about to begin. Norman Whiteside was missing from the Everton line up, having been dismissed in the last tie; the last two match-ups had produced two penalties, four goals, one sending off and nine bookings. Joe Royle was looking to win the game and you couldn't be more positive than playing with three defenders and five players up front – it was like a throw-back to the 1960s – exciting indeed and what a gamble, and what a prospect. It was an extremely windy day which would affect both teams.

Everton took first blood when Tony Cottee put them ahead as early as the 12th minute. The ball had been played through by McDonald and, as Jon Hallworth came out to try to smother the shot, the ball was chipped over his diving body into the net. It was Cottee's sixth goal of the season. McDonald went from hero to zero in the 33rd minute when he made a suicide backpass that Roger Palmer intercepted. Neville Southall came out to gather the ball but Palmer slid in and the ball bounced off the keeper onto Palmer's outstretched leg and went under Southall and rolled into the back of the net. The half time score was 1-1.

Athletic were attacking their favourite Chaddy End for the second half. Early in this half, Kevin Ratcliffe slipped and Palmer put a great centre over which Rick Holden dived at but failed to connect correctly so a chance to be 2-1 up was lost. Minutes later another chance was scorned when Neil Redfearn blasted well over the crossbar from the six yard line. This was followed by a long range special from Denis Irwin which Southall tipped over the bar. The score was still 1-1 after 90 minutes so extra time was again needed. Oldham could have done without this as they had played three times since the last encounter while Everton had only had one game.

Palmer put Ian Marshall through and he was taken down on the inside edge of the penalty area to win a penalty. It was that man McDonald who did the damage again when there was really no need as Marshall was running away from the goals. Marshy was quickly up though when he remembered that he had to take the kick which eventually won the match. Andy Ritchie, the regular penalty taker, was not playing. Marshy blasted the ball home to the left of Southall to send Boundary Park crazy with excitement. It was Marshall's first goal from the penalty spot. Cottee could have brought the visitors level minutes later had it not been for a tremendous save from Hallworth.

The Latics were 2-1 up at the end of the first period of extra time. Could they hold out for the last 15 minutes? Although every player was physicall drained they continued to attack the Everton defence and at times were lining up to take pot-shots at Southall. They did manage to hold out for a deserved win and would now face Aston Villa on the following Wednesday in the quarter-finals. The games just continued to mount up for the Latics, who were now becoming known as the 'Peoples' Favourite' as they became almost the whole of the country's second 'best team' – such was the interest built up by this team of so called cast-offs!

After the second replay Jimmy Hill said that in the turn around period of extra time it showed that Colin Harvey was under tremendous pressure as he was having a real go at his players to get the job done. Conversely, Joe Royle was laughing and joking with his players as if it was an afternoon cup of tea time. The tension combined with the pressure on Everton to win had an adverse effect to the way that they played and, in this case, it was that pressure that shaped the result.

Latics fan, Phil Taylor, remembers, *"We had reached the 5th round of the FA Cup for the first time since 1979 and we were already in the League Cup semis. With the pinch-me season very much in the swing now, our cup form had started to be replicated in the league. We were playing two games a week and, as I was going to all of them at the time, I seemed to be forever queuing outside Boundary Park for match tickets or getting someone else to do it for me as I was off to some far flung outlet watching the 'Boys in Blue.' The Chaddy End was rocking and there were some minor scuffles as Everton fans appeared in small groups, but nothing too bad. For the first time in months, the Latics didn't seem to be able to lift themselves to the heights required to match First Division opposition and we 2-0 behind at half time. With the season going as it was, I hadn't necessarily ruled out the miracles like beating Arsenal but it didn't look good. In the second half the lads managed to raise their game and we managed to pull the two goals back to take them back to Goodison."*

"Another trip to the ground for my intended, she managed to obtain the last ticket for the Park End stand as we were only given the upper tier (about 3,000), the lower tier being empty, presumably for safety purposes. That night I lost all respect for Everton – a club who I had always had a soft spot for, with them being the second team in Liverpool to the mighty Reds whilst I was growing up, except when Joe Royle was a major contributor to one Championship winning season in 1970. The 'Blue Scouse' proceeded to try and kick Oldham off the park at every opportunity, a disgraceful show by a top division side against a new-kid on the block who were treating the nation to lovely attacking football. I recall Norman Whiteside being sent off for a knee high challenge on Mike Milligan, but there were far worse challenges going on and our lads got a right kicking. Marshy put us ahead in the first half of extra time with a free header but they equalised with a penalty and it was onto a third game which was to be held on the day of the 6th round of the FA Cup. I recall my intended advising me how shocked the BBC Radio commentators had been at Everton's bully boy tactics, with Jimmy Armfield being particularly annoyed. The third tie contained none of the strong arm tactics from Everton and, although they went ahead, we turned the game around to win 2-1 so we had to tackle league leaders Aston Villa next. It really is hard to believe, especially for our younger fans, that Oldham were, at this time, the talk of the Nation."

Amusing Anecdote 8: The second replay came at a very pivotal point of my life. In the space of the three days prior to the game, I had been diagnosed with senile cataracts and had received surgery to both of my eyes. On the Wednesday morning I had gone into the Manchester Eye Hospital for the diagnosis. The doctor confirmed the case and said, *"I have good news and bad news for you!"* The good news was that they could repair the damage but the bad news was that there was a waiting list of over one year. When I explained that I was emigrating the following month he looked down at his watch and blurted out, *"What are you doing this afternoon?"* I replied, *"Nothing,"* so he responded with, *"I'll do them both this afternoon then!"*

I had to hurriedly arrange for cover for work, get my pyjamas and stuff together and get ready for the operations. He actually did one on the Wednesday and one the following day so that I wouldn't have both eyes bandaged up at once. I left the hospital on the Friday and was given strict instructions not go do any lifting or heavy work, not to go near any crowds and not to get bumped ot jostled for a couple of weeks. I was to stay at home, do nothing and just rest.

What a predicament as the Latics were playing the second Everton replay the very next day! What could I do? There was only one answer and that was 'support ther lads!' I got to the ground very early to execute a plan to find a 'quiet' place to watch the game. By a sheer stroke of luck I bumped into (not physically of course) the sergeant of police who was on duty for the game. He just happened to be one of my best friends and was the best man at my wedding, as I was also his. I explained my predicament to him and he let me into the ground and stood me directly under the floodlight pylon between the corner of the Chaddy End and the Main Stand. He also instructed officers to make sure that I didn't get disturbed by anyone. It was really hard to not jump up and down when the goals went in and especially when the final whistle went and the lads were through to the next round. I must have had about twenty imaginary black cats surrounding that particular floodlight pylon on that day!

Southampton v Oldham – League Cup Quarter-Final 1989/90 2-2.

Wednesday 24th January 1990
The Dell 7:30pm

OLDHAM		SOUTHAMPTON
Jon Hallworth	1	Tim Flowers
Dennis Irwin	2	Jason Dodd
Andy Barlow	3	Francis Benali
Nick Henry	4	Jimmy Case
Ian Marshall	5	Kevin Moore
Paul Warhurst	6	Russell Osman
Neil Adams	7	Matt Le Tissier
Andy Ritchie	8	Glenn Cockerill
Roger Palmer	9	Paul Rideout
Mike Milligan	10	Barry Horne
Rick Holden	11	Rod Wallace
Willie Donachie	12	Neil Ruddock
Scott McGarvey	14	Alan Shearer
Manager: Joe Royle		Manager: Chris Nicholl

Referee: R Milford (Bristol). Linesmen: DR Palmer;
RJ Pardowe.

Crowd: 21,026

The most annoying thing about this game is that I can't find the bloody programme for the event. I have got hundreds of the blasted things and yet I can't find this one. So I don't know who the linesmen were and can't read the pre-match rantings of Chris Nicholl, the Southampton manager. It is no good ringing up Oldham Athletic and asking them for a copy of the programme because 'Big Gordon' tells me that they have thrown them all away. Good One! I must say though that Mr Nicholl was generous in defeat following the replay at Boundary Park and said that we were in fact a good First Division side. I knew this by now and the league form was beginning to frustrate me, and yet the cup form in both competitions was sensational.

It's weird, but it has something to do with cups, in that they are special. I hate with a passion the undervaluing of our two domestic cup competitions in today's world, especially by the pidgin English speaking foreign managers, and I include the Scots in with that as well. They bring together all sorts of strange 'bedfellow' fixtures and I suppose it is the excitement and the romance up and down our country of having teams like Aldershot play Newcastle and Celtic playing Clyde that makes it just magic. And then there are, of course, 'Upsets' and 'Giant Killings' and also 'Massacres' like poor Scarborough and West Ham, but that is the inherent beauty of cups. It is the very stuff of legends that Keats would wax lyrical about and he wouldn't have to write an *Ode to a Nightingale* if there had been football when he was alive!

January was to see us play eight games, which was a large overload for that time of the season, and for this reason I think Joe decided that we should fly down to the game rather than the energy sapping bus journey that we would normally have to endure. Coach journeys were part of the team bonding bit but were hellishly inconvenient given the British Isles attention to infrastructure. No wonder the country is skint – our workers spend half the f**king man hours sitting in traffic jams. That is non-productive! Look at the M25. As soon as they built it, it filled up, and it still is! However, we did fly down for the game at the Dell and Neil Redfearn would later describe our air trips as 'Optongchoggybobba Airways' which was some kind of reference to *Dick Dasterdly*!

The side Joe picked was compromised because Dennis Irwin was injured so he played Warhurst and Marshall as centre backs and put Earl (or Aerial as Willy used to call him) at right back. Andy Barlow was a certainty at left back at that particular time. He had me and Bert on the wings and the two idiots, Nick and Milly, in the middle. Rodge and Stitch played up front. The Rooster, Captain J Hallworth, played in goals and he was superb throughout! Joe used to hate keepers but he had two great guys that he could rely on in Captain and Rhodsey. It was a good solid side and we did have on the face of it good strength in depth.

The game was fast and furious in a packed Dell which, for you young chaps, was Southampton's old ground. It was a superb little theatre and definitely a 'home advantage spinner.' It reminded me more of a cricket ground than a football stadium because it had many small and odd shaped stands like the test grounds around the World used to be. In fact they still are but I have to confess I can't understand what Lancashire are playing at with that red monstrosity that they have just built at Old Trafford. Were the committee all pissed when they sanctioned it or what?

It was a strange game in that we, in my opinion, being out there, were in control for most of the time but save a couple of efforts from me we didn't really trouble them but more just contained them. The first goal for 'The Saints' was a deflection off Earl Barrett from Le Tissier who, as per normal, would 'passenger' his way through a game and then suddenly 'tip up' and do something of eminent significance. Now I don't mind this of a player as long as his is capable of popping up and scoring every week so if he does he can be as lazy as he likes. Matt Le Tiss did just this! It's when you have lazy bastards who don't affect a game with a piece of magic that you have problems! It would be Earl who deflected the ball of course, as he was beginning to have the 'anti-Midas' touch in front of goal. For the rest of the game he was magnificent and snuffed-out, almost single-handedly, their threats. We lost Warhurst in a freak accident when he twisted his ankle by colliding with a pitch surrounding hoarding, which is what you got at these old grounds. Willy Donachie came on to act, as he did often, as a piece of mental encouragement on the field. His experience used to often guide us through closing stages of games, and he did just that on this famous night. We were heading out of the competition but when he came on it seemed to calm us down!

Our equalizer was amazing because of the construction of the goal. Nick Henry put in a cross which I would deem ineffective, but somehow Andy Ritchie reacted and planted a first time header in to the near post top corner. Their keeper, Flowers, didn't read it, but you wouldn't really when you look at it! 1-1 and heading for a draw and replay. Then they got, in my view, an outrageously generous penalty when Horne basically tangled himself up in the area and threw himself to the ground! Uncharacteristically I went over to the ref, Milford, and let him know that he had been conned and that he had cost us our future. Le Tissier took the penalty and he doesn't miss!

That was it, but we rallied and went down the other end to score a brilliant last gasp injury time equalizer in time added on that I don't know where Milford found it from. He was surrounded and berated by the Southampton players on the final whistle and I would not argue. I can only think that he felt sorry for his mistake with the penalty, but he would never concede that of course. Milly won the ball and correctly slid it out to me and I just pushed it into the area luckily through a defender's legs. Stitch threw a leg at it and it flew in off Benali and we were back on Optongchoggybobba Airways as fast as we could, ready for the replay in which we would demolish Southampton. It was a great game and again cemented our belief that we were a team!

Amusing Anecdote 9: The amusing tale from this game came on the way down to Southampton on the plane. Andy Rhodes had, and probably still has, a fear of flying and didn't relish going down to The Dell on what he considered to be a First World War biplane. He was as nervous as you could be on take-off and I was the wrong person that he could wish to be sitting alongside. I made comments like, 'well if it goes down who gives a shit, at least we will be famous!' This didn't go down well as you can imagine! After elevating to about a 1,000 feet something that looked like smoke started to fill the fuselage and Rhodesy started to 'shit himsen' as we would both say in Yorky speak. The pilot assured us all that it was just condensation coming out of the fuselage. It didn't convince any of us, least alone Rhodesy who was like a cat on a hot-tinned African roof for the one hour journey and he was the same on the way back! Joe took to flying us to quite a few southern games and I suppose, like many things around this time, it was the start of things which are now the norm. Today's teams fly from Manchester to London as a matter of habit. We went on prop shafted things. Now clubs like Man City own their 757s and have their own pilots and crew!

The Dell was packed to capacity with several thousands of supporters locked out of the sold-out match. It was particularly frustrating for the Oldham fans who had travelled so far to just stand outside and listen to the action happening on the inside! Oldham approached the game with only one defeat in their last eight games and the team had been flown down for the tie. The first half was thoroughly entertaining with the majority of play being dominated by the Latics. The fans were in fine voice with cries of 'Come on Oldham' completely drowning out the home supporters. Unfortunately, the one and only shot that the Saints managed in the first half was the one that counted. Matthew Le Tissier's strike took a wicked deflection off Earl Barrett and went past Jon Hallworth and into the net to give the Saints a half time lead.

The second half was more end-to-end but as the visitors strode forward the Saints had enough chances to 'put the tie to bed' with their counter-attacks but they did not take their opportunites. This was mostly down to Jon Hallworth who was having a cracker and fully earning his corn. Justice was done with ten minutes remaining when a cross by Nick Henry was headed home by Andy Ritchie, who continued his record of having scored in every round of the competition. It looked odds-on for another replay until Barry Horne was brought down for a penalty just five minutes from time. Le Tissier did what he does well and stroked home the spot kick, his sixth of the season, to score what looked like the winner.

The goal was heartbreaking for Athletic who had really fought back well. However, Royle's raiders refused to give in and were rewarded four minutes into injury time. With the home supporters whistling incessantly as a reminder to the referee, a low cross from Rick Holden from the left wing was met with Ritchie's outstretched leg as he slid in to break the hearts of the Southampton supporters and simultaneously send the joyous travelling Oldhamers into delectation. Ritchie wheeled away with his, now familiar, charactaristic arm aloft in celebration. It was an incredible climax to the game and Tim Flowers almost whacked the ball out of the stadium in sheer frustration. As the whistle went Ritchie went to shake Jimme Case's hand but he brushed him aside as he was so disappointed. The goal was later described as being worth a million pounds – such was the importance.

Amusing Anecdote 10: A longtime Latics' fan reported, *"I was present at the game with my young daughter. We had left in good time and arrived at the ground 45 minutes before kick off time. The ground was full so we hung around outside for a while with about 600 other Latics' fans until Southampton's lovely boys in blue came along. They were in a line with shields and told us to effin' move or else we would be in effin' nick! What a nice end to a 260 mile trip! We had to 'watch' the match by listening to the radio in the car. At the end of all the frustration though, we had the last laugh."*

After the match Joe Royle said, *"It was a just result. We deserved a draw,"* and he also claimed that the penalty was a disputed one as his lads were adamant that it wasn't a penalty. The interviewer suggested that Oldham looked like they were dead and buried when the penalty went in but Joe responded, *"We are never dead and buried. We have never been this far before so we are not going to let this chance slip."* Saints' boss Chris Nicholl, on the other hand, commented, *"Good luck to Joe Royle. He has got a tidy side there."* Not exactly full of praise but he was probably still shell-shocked like many others!

Oldham supporter 'Fryatt' best summed up the game as, *"On a personal note, this was my favourite away game ever. Mumps railway station, early morning, I travelled on our hired football special. There were 500 Latics fans on board and one poor sod had brought 30 cans of ale for the trip, only for the police to tell him that it must all be drunk before embarking. Twenty, or so, of us helped the poor lad out! I was totally taken aback at out support that evening. It seemed that 70% of out regular home attendance had made the long journey south as well over 2,000 had travelled for the night game at the other end of the country. As the away end was full some 30 minutes before kick-off many of the supporters were locked out of the ground. Many were totally dejected as they had decided to 'duck' two days off work. I just about made it into the ground and the term 'you couldn't swing a cat' came to mind when I saw the crush of supporters. With 89 minutes played and 2-1 down we had more than held our own against a side who were fourth in the First Division. I honestly thought that our fantastic run was finally coming to an end. With the Saints fans blowing for the final whistle my thoughts were, 'One last big effort please lads.' A cross came into the box and it happened! Andy Ritchie slid in to score a remarkable goal, a heartbreaking one for the Saints, but I must confess that that 60 seconds was better than sex! I finished the game crushed at the bottom of the terrace with a 60-odd-year-old bloke. We embraced each other like father and son even though we had never clapped eyes on each other before. That was real football passion. We both agreed that it was our year for Wembley as we knew we would win the replay. That night heaven landed on the south coast of England!"*

Amusing Anecdote 11: A lady living close to the ground had a phone number which was very similar to the Athletic main phone number; it was one number different. She was inundated with calls for the club and was constantly answering the phone all day for enquiries about replay tickets and she was regularly having to redirect callers to the correct number. Personally, I think she should have asked the club for commission on sales. She could have retired early.

Oldham v Aston Villa – FA Cup Quarter-Final 1989/90 3-0.

Wednesday 14th March 1990
Boundary Park 7:30pm

OLDHAM		ASTON VILLA
Jon Hallworth	1	Nigel Spink
Dennis Irwin	2	Chris Price
Andy Barlow	3	Kevin Gage
Nick Henry	4	Paul McGrath
Earl Barrett	5	Stuart Gray
Paul Warhurst	6	Kent Nielsen
Neil Redfearn	7	Tony Daley
Roger Palmer	8	David Platt
Ian Marshall	9	Ian Olney
Mike Milligan	10	Gordon Cowans
Rick Holden	11	Bernie Gallacher
Neil Adams	12	Paul Birch
Scott McGarvey	14	Mark Blake
Manager: Joe Royle		Manager: Graham Taylor

Referee: K Hackett (Sheffield). Linesmen: DS Oliver (Darlington); J Ross (Northumberland).

Crowd: 19,490

Aston Villa came full of confidence and were expecting to progress to the semi-finals of the FA Cup. I had never played against them before but had watched them a couple of years earlier at Bradford City when they were a second division side. That was the year that they stormed the league under the management of Graham Taylor, and very impressed I was with them too. I was particularly taken with Alan McInally whose power and movement was second to none and he destroyed Bradford on that cold Saturday afternoon back in early 1988. I was able to watch games around that period of my life as I played for Halifax who played many Friday night games. This freed up Saturday afternoons to be able to go and watch games.

Graham Taylor was soon to become England manager and had an impressive record of producing direct no-nonsense football at Watford and then Villa. He favoured a long ball, but once in the final third he liked to use wingers to cross early balls into the danger areas which was similar to us in a way, only we mixed up a long ball with short interpassing in the midfield. There is a lot of crap talked in football which lends itself to snobbery and the taking of moral high-ground when it comes to the philosophy of the long and short game. It doesn't really matter how you get the ball into the final third, but with the long ball you have to be bloody good at it because retaining a long punt down the field for a flick on means you are gambling with winning back possession again, and against good teams you might not win the ball back. You need a lightning-quick centre forward and dumb defences and I could not believe how effective this was when I joined Watford.

Luther Blissett used to just gamble in behind, for instance, big Dave Bamber's flick-on and he would latch on to the end of knock downs with amazing regularity. He was, as I have intimated, helped by stupid defenders getting caught out by one flick on. When it doesn't work it is awful to watch and proponents of this philosophy tend to overkill the use of this tactic to the extent of instructing their players to always look long. By the same token, the so called short passing game 'purists' can create mind-numbing boring play by overkill on possession and the crowds in Britain soon get hacked off if the ball is knocked around at the back for more than 30 seconds.

Watching Colombia play in the late 80s early 90s was tedious, they just kept the ball in endless weaving patterns orchestrated by Carlos Valderamma and they almost refused to attack. Good sides like the Brazil of 1970 used to do both of course. They would knock the ball around until they saw an opportunity to hit the ball long into a runners path and it would be accurate enough, and the recipient would be skilful enough, to retain possession. So endeth the philosophy!

Aston Villa thus came to Boundary Park with more than a little direct philosophy but it just did not work against our back four who I am glad to say were not dummies, but when they occasionally got it wrong they had enough pace to extricate themselves from the situation. Occasionally Willie Donachie, our forward-thinking, if a little eccentric, coach would have a sprinting competition where we all had to line up along the goal line and sprint to the 18 yard line. The fastest were in a league of their own and consisted of Paul Warhurst, Earl Barrett and Ian Marshall. Craig Fleming, when he joined us later on, would be in this bracket. Next in line would be Dennis Irwin, Roger Palmer and Neil Adams and then you were into the half way lot of me Milly, Nick Henry Andy Barlow, Stitch, Bunny and Redders. The keepers would always be last. I was in effect half way down the field but that didn't matter because I was as quick as any over five yards which is all I needed to get a cross or shot in, and the same went for Andy Ritchie and Neil Redfearn. Pace is wonderful to have but you also needed brains.

I have lost count of how many young lads, like Rod Thomas at Watford, who were pure lightning, but when they got to the by-line they crossed it behind the goal. There was an element of composure missing. Tony Daly for Aston Villa fitted into this category and I am sure that on this particular evening, if we had opened the stadium gates he would have dribbled the ball out of the ground and around Rochdale Market before he realised where he was! In effect, Villa posed no threat whatsoever on the night and when I lashed one in from 20 yards or so they just '*went.*' The ball was played into one of our strikers, Rodge, I think by Andy Barlow and I just went round the corner inside to gather it, took one touch and hit it goalwards. I bought a raffle ticket and won! I felt the best I have ever felt on a football pitch on that night and gave my full back, Chris Price, a torrid evening and he ended up a quivering wreck by the end!

Rick Holden's 20 yarder which stunned Villa

Villa had a goodish team without being outstanding and undoubtedly their best players were Paul McGrath, David Platt and Gordon Cowans. McGrath had known injury problems which meant that he didn't train but played the odd game, and Platt was in the England frame and went on to star in the 1990 World Cup but on the evidence of his contribution against us you wouldn't have given him a second glance. He was totally ineffective! Gordon Cowans was a legend in Villa's history, having won the European Cup, and should have commanded respect. But up and coming players do not respect the past when they are playing, and a misplaced comment from Cowans to Neil Redfearn caused a response that I couldn't believe. Redders asked him if he had had his nose thrown on, in reference to Cowan's nose being rather large and spread. I was shocked but that was football then. Imagine it today – Redders would be locked up if Cowans had squealed like they do now!

Chris Price had tried to put in a hard challenge on me early on; I suspect with the idea that it would put me off if he hurt me. But I did the wingers best trick to get his own back on the full back, which is to knock the ball past him and then let him have possession. He then makes the mistake of trying to shield it out of play by doing that classic 'obstruction manoeuvre' which referees never pick up on. I find that is out of order! Anyway, it just allows the winger to take a free swipe which I did and wrote him off into the hoardings. That was one each, and put an end to his game!

At half time the atmosphere in the dressing room was strangely calm and subdued which I put down to the game being easy and we knew that if we went about things properly we would beat them without problems. In the second half Marshy frightened Price into a mistake which resulted in an own goal from a back pass. Marshy bore down on him like a cave man from the Neander Valley and panicked Price into a hurried back pass which slid past the advancing and bewildered Spink! Well you would panic wouldn't you with Marshy about to write you off? The fans in the Chaddy Road end were making a great noise and I think that they contributed to Price shitting himself and panicking also! Then it got worse for Price when I twisted him and megged him before hitting a low shot at Spink. I didn't catch it as I liked but that made it bobble and Spink could only parry it into Redder's path who calmly tapped it in and that was game over!

Villa were destroyed and Graham Taylor, their manager, was left only to lavish praise on our players. He had no choice and the following year he showed us ultimate respect by coming to coach us for a session as leaders of the second division to see for himself our quality. The win against Villa was the peak of our season and, in my opinion, after this we began to fatigue. If we had played the semi-final of the FA Cup the following week and the final of the League Cup the week after that we would have won. But the games were stacking up and they eventually told and we wouldn't capture top form until start of the next season. What we did do was show the British public who we were and what we were all about, and it was up to us to become more consistent in league football. We had to transfer our cup form into winning the division which was still our priority.

Amusing Anecdote 12: My anecdote for this particular match involves what happened a year later. The former Villa manager was now the newly installed England boss. He came to see us as potential England players and put on a session to evaluate and confirm if what he had witnessed in his night of destruction was a one-off display of skill and understanding. Following what was a fairly ordinary session in which we had all seen before he asked us for our feedback to which Marshy retorted, much to Joe's jaw clanging amazement, that it was 'fookin roobish' and turned around and walked away. Result – much hilarity, both squirmed and laughed-out-loud stuff echoing across the training ground. Could that be the reason why Marshy never played for England?

The manager's pre-match notes were full of praise for his lads. He said, *"There barely seems time to get our breath these days as we stagger on from big game to big game. Our club, that has been totally bereft of cup history until this season, now finds itself rubbing shoulders with the elite of British football with only tonight's opposition Aston Villa, barring our path to a semi-final with our neighbours from Manchester United. I found myself in one of the local 'watering holes' Saturday night, surrounded by cheering, singing and disbelieving fans, one of whom just kept nodding his head and saying, 'pinch me.' It occurred to me that if this season needed a motto, or a title, then 1989/90 should definitely go down as the 'pinch me' season!"* That saying certainly stuck alright!

It was another windy night, coupled with another capacity crowd. The only change in the team from Saturday was that Paul Warhurst had replaced Neil Adams. Oldham applied all the early pressure as well as having all the best chances, and they were in no way overawed by their illustrious First Division counterparts, who had entered the match as First Division leaders. The 38th minute strike by Rick Holden was one to savour. Roger Palmer played a key role in the goal and it rattled in off the underside of the crossbar to give Spink no chance. It was Holden's eighth goal of the season and what a cracker!

The second half began with the Latics attacking their favourite Chaddy Road End, and in the knowledge that they had now scored in 36 consecutive home matches, of which 23 had been won and 12 were drawn. An early move by Warhurst, from a Holden corner, resulted in him threading the ball through on goal. With Marshall chasing, the ball struck Price on the knee and was deflected past the keeper for an own goal. As soon as I saw that ball hit the back of the net I knew that we had won another! There would be no way back for the Villa. The feeling in the Chaddy End was absolutely electric and there was almost a permanent smile on all of the fan's faces. You just had to be there to experience it as words can't really describe it!

Platt got a good chance to pull one back but Jon Hallworth got down quickly to snuff out the threat. He had almost been a spectator up to that point. Half way through the second half the match was sealed. Holden nutmegged the hapless Price, made a brilliant run into the box, and hit the ball goalwards. It bobbled and Spink could only parry the ball into the path of Neil Redfearn who must have thought 'thank you very much' as he had the easiest of tap-ins to make it 3-0. At this stage the crowd began in unison with, *"We want seven... We want seven..."* Oh, what an embarrassment for the Villa players, staff and fans! It's almost criminal to do that to the League leaders but it was so enjoyable! We were an unblievable team! Price had another go at Holden who had given him a torrid time and brought another foul in favour of the Latics. The humour flowed yet again from the fans with, *"Just because you're losing!"* and, *"are you watching Manchester?"* in reference to the upcoming match on 8th April.

The Latics were in the FA Cup semi-finals for only the second time, the last one being back in 1913 when they were knocked out by...... Aston Villa! Joe Royle commented, *"The two little lads in midfield never gave them breathing space and we never game their centre-half a minutes peace."* When questioned about running out of steam he continued, *"They are not doing a lot of training. They are drinking more champagne than doing training!"*

This was followed up with the *Daily Express* interview on Thursday 15th March 1990 under the headline of 'Right Royle Party.' Big Joe said, *"This victory has to rank as high as any of* the teams we have knocked out in the cup runs this season. My players keep shining and look Division One class but the only way they can prove it is by getting into the division and playing at that level." Rick Holden had always reiterated that sentiment and said, "The cup runs, as great as they were, were just a mild and enthusiastic distraction which had the value of building confidence for the players and the fans alike. It wasn't my goal at all!"

Graham Taylor described the pitch as 'a red herring' and preferred to concentrate more on praising his opposition. He graciously stated, "Look at the Oldham side. They are very competitive, they know what they are doing and they are confident in every area. The biggest thing is that they get that ball into areas that hurt you, irrespective of the surface, that doesn't even come into it. Their policy is the way that they play, and I'm sure that they try to play that way away from home as well as at home.... and it will bring them results as it has done!"

Oldham had by this stage come through no less than fifteen cup ties, including replays, and had disposed of First Division opposition in Arsenal, Southampton, Everton and Aston Villa. Next up would be neighbours Manchester United. The club were fast becoming everyone's favourite team as the big guns were constantly being shot down. Rick Holden had openly declared that part of their success was the fact that they had no 'miserable southerners' in the team but even the 'miserable southerners' were starting to smile at the exploits of the proudly northern based team. Reporters were seriously in danger of running out of descriptive expressions as each cup game climaxed. If anyone could have invented a new lexicon of superlatives specifically for the Latics they could have been made for life, without *Dragon's Den!*

Fryatt described the result as, "One of the best displays I have witnessed from a Latics side as we battered one of the best sides in the country at the time. After a great finish by 'tricky' Ricky Holden, Villa just crumbled. The home fans were singing, 'We've got a bye to the semis,' as they already knew that they would be playing Manchester United."

Oldham v Manchester United – FA Cup Semi-Final 1989/90 3-3.

Sunday 8th April 1990
Maine Road 3:30pm

OLDHAM		MANCHESTER UNITED
Jon Hallworth	1	Jim Leighton
Dennis Irwin	2	Lee Martin
Andy Barlow	3	Colin Gibson
Nick Henry	4	Steve Bruce
Earl Barrett	5	Mike Phelan
Andy Holden	6	Gary Pallister
Neil Redfearn	7	Brian Robson
Andy Ritchie	8	Paul Ince
Ian Marshall	9	Brian McClair
Mike Milligan	10	Mark Hughes
Rick Holden	11	Neil Webb
Paul Warhurst	12	Mark Robins
Roger Palmer	14	Danny Wallace
Manager: Joe Royle		Manager: Alex Ferguson

Referee: J Worrall (Warrington). Linesmen: DG Frampton (Poole); JS Sinclair (Durham).

Crowd: 44,026

This was the biggest game in Oldham's recent history and one that the whole nation was waiting for. It was scheduled to follow the earlier game of Liverpool v Crystal Palace which kicked off at lunch time and turned out to be an incredible game in which Palace overcame all the odds and triumphed 4-3. We watched it in the clubhouse before travelling down to Maine Road for our game. Palace's victory did create a negative vibe or two within the camp because we thought that it was unlikely that our game would be as thrilling as that game and the likelihood of a second giant killing act on the same day was less realistic.

We were in the away dressing room which suited us because it gave us that feeling of it being an away fixture which we had come to enjoy. We liked the siege mentality and the 'them against us' feeling and it made us underdogs even more. We quickly got on top and I should have scored early on but just couldn't get there, other than to force a corner at the near post at the away end where all our supporters were.

What has always annoyed me about this chain of events is the commentary on the game by Barry Davis, that constant pain in the rear, when it came to asinine comments! After six minutes we had scored but prior to this Davis had said 'and here is Holden, who some people think holds the key to this game but he hasn't found the door yet!' – or words to that effect. I mean, the dopey twonk. The game was just six minutes old when I re-collected my miss-hit corner and, once I had wrong-footed Bryan Robson, my cross resulted in Earl slotting home our first goal. 1-0 after 6 minutes. I had unlocked the door with the key, straight away. Davis said nothing!

We were comfortable and stretching United who were really struggling to come to terms with our pressure and passing game. On the half hour mark we got caught out by a straight forward ball down the middle from Webb to Robson who slid the ball over Captain Hallworth for the equalizer. Joe had decided to play my namesake, Andy Holden, at centre-half who had been out for a long time with a knee injury. I just don't think he was fit, pace wise, no matter how hard he had worked in training. It was his first game for months and I don't think we would have conceded that goal if Warhurst had being playing – because of his sheer pace. That was my opinion, but Joe had opted to use Andy for his strength against Hughes and he certainly had a great game overall. It just shows you how difficult it is when it comes to management decisions and sometimes you just can't win.

We had the better of the chances but it remained 1-1 until the break and the feeling in the dressing room was that United were there for the taking but we had to cut out the mistakes which we felt was the only way we would lose. And so it turned out be, because their second goal was basically a fluke. It came from an innocuous cross from Wallace which cannoned off Neil Webb's face and flew into the net. It was a stroke of luck which Webb knew little about. We responded with a great goal when Redders and Denis Irwin played each other in, and the resultant cross was hammered in by Marshy with a great first-time right footed volley. Marshy was as two footed as was Denis and Redders, but it was only Denis who played international football, for Ireland. When one considers that Neil Webb won England caps and Redders didn't, and Hughes and McClair were for Wales and Scotland, it is just a shame that Marshy wasn't Irish!

Extra time came and United scored another scraggy goal, and again down the middle, which was seriously poor defending and another slice of bad luck. Wallace latched onto a ball down the middle and miss-hit his shot past Captain. I couldn't believe it! We were playing against 'Lady Luck' and had to carve out another great goal. This time it was Milly who fed Marshy; he played a devastating first time cross into the box for Roger Palmer to tap home. It was a great goal. Apart from a Robin's header which was well saved by Captain we had all the best play and chances. In the last few seconds I should have won it for us, but my right footed shot from the edge of the box clipped the outside of the post with Leighton well beaten. I should have run it into the box and made sure but I think I was just too tired and tried to catch them with a long range dig. It was a sickener and we had to settle for a replay even though we were the better side, but that is fooball and Manchester United have always had the ability to dig in when playing below par! In the dressing room we were a little deflated and then we went down into the bar to meet our relatives.

Amusing Anecdote 13: When we went to the bar something really funny happened. We approached the players' bar but the bar steward, who was dressed like a Beefeeter, on the door wouldn't let us, the Oldham players, into the room because we didn't have passes. Steve Bruce turned up and asked us what was happening and we told him that we were barred from entering because of the old officious tw*t on the door dressed like a 'Chelsea Pensioner.' Bruce rounded on him and pushed the bloke out of the way and we all filed in. Brucey was great and said words like 'these lads have just played in the semi-final of the FA Cup and deserve a drink, now get out of the way!' Class act!

The replay was a game too far being only three days after the first tie, and we were tired during extra time (or at least I was) and I lost Phelan for his run forward to cross for their winner. I was devastated about this as I had cost us another replay! We should have won in normal time though because Nick Henry had a perfectly good goal ruled out when his shot clearly went over the line after hitting the bar from 22 yards. Another miscarriage of justice in the crazy world of 'Head-in-the-Sand Professional Football' for not embracing technology and, remarkably and scandalously, it still goes on today!

We had to lick our wounds and watch United beat Crystal Palace after a replay in the final at Wembley which was more spawn and resilience from United. We would have beaten all sides if it had all happened a month earlier but the games had taken their toll and we had played more games than any other professional side in Britain during the 1989/90 season. It was a sad end to our FA Cup game but we had proved that we were as good as anybody!

This was 'the biggie' as far as the fans were concerned and, contrary to what my mates were insinuating, I was not present to witness the last time the Latics were in an FA Cup semi-final! The build up to the game was astronomic and all the local radio stations were talking about nothing else but the match-up. I used to listen to *Sweeney's Sixties Classics* on *Piccadilly Radio* as the DJ, Mike Sweeney, used to host the show and was regularly seen at Boundary Park. He often confessed to being a Latics fan and he even trained with the team for some time, although it was also known that he was a Reds supporter. It caused many fans, from both teams, to phone the station to get him to stop 'sitting on the fence' and officially declare his allegiance. As the game approached he had no other option than to admit which team he wanted to win the semi-final – he opted for United and lost a lot of listeners in the process. He was officially a Manc!

It was Oldham's 54th match of the season and their 16th in cup competitions but the Latics had lost three league games in the build up to this match. 'Big Joe' reminisced in his pre-match programme preamble and said, *"If you would have told me that I would spend my 41st birthday watching my team compete with the mighty Manchester United in the semi-final of English soccer's most prestigious cup competition, I would have sent for the little yellow van and the men with the straight-jacket."* He was just 90 minutes away from joining that elite band of managers who have led out a team in TWO Wembley finals in the same season. When he took over from Jimmy Frizzell in July 1982 he recalled, *"It was very much unchartered territory, both for me and Oldham Athletic. It was my first job in soccer management and quite frankly I didn't know whether I would sink or swim. It was for that reason that my first contract at Boundary Park was for one year only. Winning at all cost will never be Oldham Athletic's policy as long as I am their manager. I want my team to give the paying customer value for money. How we play is every bit as important as what we achieve. More than anything I want the team to show the crowd at Maine Road and the millions watching on television that we can play soccer as it was meant to be played. I don't go in for predictions, all I will say is that I have never sent a team out yet thinking we were going to lose."*

For once, I don't remember going for a booze before the game but I do remember walking past some pubs near Maine Road: perhaps it was some kind of a self-preservation instinct that kicked-in to prevent me going for a drink; perhaps the pubs were shut because it was a Sunday! It was a nice sunny day and what I do recollect was the electric atmosphere felt as we got inside the ground and the collective feeling of anticipation among the Oldham faithful; it was a party atmosphere but with some trepidation. We couldn't wait for the excitement to begin and Maine Road was bursting at the seams.

It was end-to-end stuff and not for the feint-hearted judging by the tackles which were flying about. After some good work on the right by Rick Holden, Earl Barrett slid in to put the Latics ahead after only six minutes gone. Andy Barlow had played his part too by making Jim Leighton take his eye off the ball. The Oldham fans just went wild and were proudly singing, *"We can play on grass as well."* The first half was a no holds barred affair and Brian Robson, just back from injury, received a severe ticking-off from the referee after he had brought down Barrett after his fantastic challenge. You could sense that United were becoming more uncomfortable as the time whittled away and the Latics were still 1-0 ahead; the Oldham fans became more happy the more they sensed United's discomfort. If they could just see out the half with the score remaining at 1-0 it would breed confidence for the second half as the Latics were full value for their lead; the Reds had failed to find any sort of rhythm. The Latics were like terriers and were winning 90% of the 50-50 balls. With the half running out Robson slipped in to level the scores and bring an air of despondency to the Oldham followers who had watched their team do so well. There was no slackening of pace and Henry had a shot kicked off the line by Paul Ince but the teams left the field level.

The second half got under way with everything to play for. The Latics had shown that they had the appetite in the first half and surely it would continue. The constant cry of, *"Come on Oldham,"* continued to emanate from the fans as their soldiers got back to the field of combat. Mike Milligan displayed an exceptional piece of skill as he turned and outwitted a United player but he was unceremoniously brought down with a tackle which would have brought an automatic yellow card with todays players – but the men of those days got on with the job on instead of rolling around on the floor like a bunch of schoolgirls. In fairness to the referee, he did allow play to continue and allowed advantages to take preference over stopping play for free kicks. It contributed to the game and allowed teams to build up momentum, a trait sadly lacking today; games can no longer flow. It would be interesting to actually clock the time of the ball 'in play' today and compare it to a game in 1990.

It was a more evenly matched game in the second half. After a collision between Ian Marshall and Leighton, the keeper was required to change his shorts. He just whipped them off of the field and put on a new pair if full view of all, and shorts were short at that time! After both players had recovered, they shook hands and played on – another example of how things have changed. Webb wend down in the box after being bundled over by Andy Barlow but the referee refused to award a penalty. It didn't stop Ince from constantly chirping away at the official. It was getting on my nerves, never mind the referee and linesmen!

The Athletic fans got shook up when Webb put United ahead in the 73rd minute as they did not deserve to be behind. I felt that sickening feeling in my stomach but we had come back before so surely we could do it again, couldn't we? It took Marshall just a few minutes to redress the score and it was all smiles on the terraces again. Game on! The cry of, *"We're on the march with Royle's army, we're all going to Wembley,"* resonated around the ground. It should have been game over minutes later when Marshall broke away. 'If only' he had passed to Ritchie instead of shooting... 'If only' ...... the game is full of 'If only's.'

The last five minutes was all pressure from Oldham and it ended with the dreaded extra time. The fans couldn't ever complain about getting value for money, not that season anyway. Jimmy Hill commented at the end of full time, *"Oldham had been the most complete team and they kept their shape better, and they kept their form better than United."* United had previously maintained the knack of squeezing a goal in when needed to get through their cup games and the supporters could only wonder if it was going to happen again. Athletic had not deserved to lose the game over the 90 minutes and Marshall almost found the net in the early stages of extra time but his effort was kicked off the line.

Wallace knocked the stuffing out of the Latics supporters when he put the Reds 3-2 ahead. Was history repeating itself as United had won all their cup games by the odd goal! After the goal, Royle made his last throw of the dice by substituting Ritchie with Palmer, both players being masters of football escapology. The Latics seemed to wilt after the goal, it could have been fatigue, it could have been despondency, it could have been a combination of both, but it still wasn't over yet. So often they had clawed back in the dying embers of a game. In a last ditch effort Redfearn was pushed forward to create more chances and to rub salt in the wounds the united fans began so sing, *"Are you watching Liverpool?"* in reference to the earlier game which saw Crystal Palace overcome the scousers by 4-3.

The Latics were to have the last laugh of the afternoon though when Palmer stopped the singing by ghosting in to make a final score of 3-3 on the day. On a personal note, I was devastated as I was unable to watch the replay. As the teams confronted each other again, I was high above the Atlantic Ocean on my way to Vancouver, BC, Canada, for one of those 'have to do' decisions that life throws up. It was no consolation whatever that I missed such a poor game!

Fryatt gave his account of the day as, *"I sat in the main stand at Maine Road and it was great just to witness the Latics competing against their fat-cat neighbours. After an Earl Barrett opener we found ourselves again 2-1 down with time running out. Once again, the Latics defied all the odds and and just would not go under as Ian Marshall had other ideas. He put the Second Division side level just as time was running out to take the game, once more, to extra time. At 3-2 to United, and with extra time running out, it looked like the Latics were not destined for a second trip to Wembley in the same season. However, that black ghost known as Roger Palmer stole in to make it 3-3 at the death. Just to see the United fans, with their hands up to their faces and trying to hang on for a replay, was absolutely priceless!"*

Oldham v Nottingham Forest – League Cup Final 1989/90 0-1.

Sunday 29th April 1990
Wembley Stadium 3:00pm

OLDHAM		NOTTINGHAM FOREST
Andy Rhodes	1	Steve Sutton
Dennis Irwin	2	Brian Laws
Andy Barlow	3	Stuart Pearce
Nick Henry	4	Des Walker
Earl Barrett	5	Steve Chettle
Paul Warhurst	6	Steve Hodge
Neil Adams	7	Gary Crosby
Andy Ritchie	8	Garry Parker
Frankie Bunn	9	Nigel Clough
Mike Milligan	10	Nigel Jemson
Rick Holden	11	Franz Carr
Roger Palmer	12	Terry Wilson
Gary Williams	14	Tommy Gaynor
Manager: Joe Royle		Manager: Brian Clough

Referee: J Martin (Hampshire). Linesmen: JB Cox (Crewkerne); D Frampton (Poole)

Crowd: 74,343

I have never watched this game on video because it pissed me off so much that we lost! I know you have to lose sometime but when I looked back years later I thought that maybe we would have been better off losing in the first round rather than in the final. But then, retrospectively, I dismiss my negative thoughts because you could never forgo the experience of being in these games and the fans would never swap a final for a first round exit. It also inspired me to become a winner and there is nothing like the feeling of defeat to inspire one to victory.

The thing was that we went down on the Saturday and had just the one night's stay before the final. This was a bit naive because we didn't get a good night's sleep, or at least I didn't, because I was thinking about the final all the time and the experience of Wembley. We turned up at the stadium and lost lots of nervous energy drinking in the atmosphere and it was almost like a celebration game rather than a hard bitten league or cup game elsewhere. We should have gone down two or three days earlier and visited the place before hand to get to know the setup . This is what Andy Ritchie and I made sure of when we took the Barnsley lads to the Millenium Stadium the night before the play-off final against Swansea in 2006, so that they could take pictures and videos and get a feel of the place.

The other factors that I make excuses for was the temperature, as it was roasting, and the game differential between the two teams. We were playing our 61st game of the season whereas Forest were nowhere near that volume and were thus fresher! This makes one hell of a difference at professional level and this, together with Forest's experience of playing at Wembley, and the heat, took the edge off the ability to run the opposition ragged, which I know we would have done if we had played the game at Hartlepool two months earlier. We proved we were a better side 18 months later, when we beat them at Boundary Park in the First Division.

Other things happened too which, on other days, would have helped our luck. Their keeper, Sutton, had a blinder and made a couple of unbelievable saves and two balls flew across the six-yard-box; how Roger or Bert didn't get a final touch to knock it into the net I will never know so it just wasn't our day!

In the dressing room at half time, we were sitting there knackered, hot and sweating our bollocks off, and most of the lads had their shirts off. We were pouring cold water on our heads to try to cool down and I changed my shirt because it was so heavy with sweat. Joe asked that one of us should go out and make a name for ourself by scoring the winner, but it was Nigel Jemson who did that when he collected his own rebounded shot off Rhodesy and knocked it into the net for the only goal.

We pushed and pushed but they had had the luck at both ends of the pitch and it just didn't happen. I hated the whole experience and was as mad as hell because it just felt like a massive let down. I couldn't get out of the place quickly enough and then we had to endure a blasted reception at a minging Northampton hotel on the way home. I also couldn't understand this (preparation wise), because we had a league game at home to Oxford United in less than 48 hours as we were trying to play catch up due to our fixture backlog. I thought we still had a chance of reaching the play-offs and I just wanted to be at home in bed because I was knackered and yawning all through the evening reception; we got home at something like 1.30am. It was a day off on the Monday but I went in to train with Billy Urmson and the kids, to sweat the shite I had eaten and drunk out of my system, ready for Oxford. It worked as I scored my only Football League hat-trick as we beat Oxford 4-1 and we also redeemed some pride and got ourselves a chance to get into the play-offs. We needed to salvage something from the season and we had another massive game that we needed to win at home on the Thursday, again just 48 hours later.

At the hotel in the nothingness that is Northampton, things started to get out of hand because once the ale got in, the wit quickly went west, and Marshy lost his rag! Marshy had been forced to make the biggest decision of his life (football-wise that is) which was whether to risk a cortisone injection in his thigh for a strain or to avoid it and miss the final! Marshy was clearly upset by something. My guess was that it was the same feeling that I had, which was one of deep resentment at dominating a competition from the start to five yards from the finishing line, only to come second – which at Wembley is like coming last. It manifested itself in Marshy ripping a toilet door off in anger during an argument with Joe. Joe had to fend him off with a chair! The reality of the occasion was that we had failed and we were all really pissed off by it, and yet the club seemed to be happy. They thought that they had achieved something and basked in the glory of failure because it had made money and a reputation. It meant nothing to me and still doesn't except for being able to play at Wembley!

In 2011, the powers that be, probably Alan Hardy and Gordon Lawton, decided to celebrate 20 years since Wembley and had a big do at the Town Hall which also coincided with the annual awards of the club such as the 'Player of the Year' and all that bullshit! When I asked as to why we were celebrating failure and as to why we weren't having a party to celebrate winning the Championship in 1992, the question was met with deafening silence. They even cocked it up by not organizing a late bar! They couldn't back then, and they still can't organise piss-ups. Anyway, it was a great game for the fans because it was our first visit to Wembley and everyone had a great day out but for me. It was a huge anti-climax because we lost but it made me more determined than ever to become a winner and I am going to let Dave spend most of the words on this game!

Well I must admit that I was saddened, and somewhat shocked, at Rick's confessions of his feelings in the summing up of this great game. I can totally understand the disappointment of a player not winning the game but it is sorrowful to think that he was harbouring all his despair while the fans, whom he had given so much pleasure to, were enjoying themselves. I too felt down in the dumps as I stood, thoughtfully, looking at the empty Wembley field at the end of the game, but for me, the anti-climax of defeat on the day did not dispel the the unique feeling of exhilaration which had been brought about by the miraculous journey which had taken the little Latics from the Pennine Way all the way to Wembley Way.

The journey for me had been an exceptionally long one. I was in the process of emigrating to Canada and, as my visa was about to expire, it meant that I could not delay my trip over there – I had to be in Canada on 22nd April at the latest and the match was just one week later! I had vowed to myself that I would never go to Wembley until I could watch my own team and I honestly thought it would never happen. As soon as the Latics qualified for the final I went to a travel agent in Lees village and said, *"I would like to book a return flight to England from Canada please."* The agent corrected, *"Don't you mean to Canada from England?"* When I explained the reason why, she soon accommodated my request. I had only been in Canada for a couple of weeks before I was back in Oldham.

My story hit the front page of the *Ashton Advertiser* with a photo article, there was a *John Gaunt* column article in the *Oldham Evening Chronicle* and *Granada TV* made a programme about Oldham for which I was interviewed, regarding my devotion to the Latics. They all mentioned the fact that I was travelling to Oldham, instead of London, so that I could travel down to London on the supporters coach just to savour the atmosphere. They also mentioned the fact that it had cost £400 for the flight and that I had reserved £200 for beer – but I probably exceeded that limit! I returned back to Canada on 1st May. The TV programme was never aired due to the fact that Oldham Rugby failed in their semi-final tie and didn't make it to Wembley. It would have been the rugby final on the Saturday, followed by the League Cup Final on the Sunday, both represented by Oldham teams – the town would have been a ghost town!

The build up to the match was nothing short of phenominal. The whole town was talking about the match, local newspapers were giving away pull-out suppliments, all the headlines were about the big match, local radio stations were doing interviews, the TV stations were discussing the upcoming final and the Littlewoods Store in Oldham had a full window display with the actual Littlewood's Cup. The cup was surrounded by an exhibition of several manikins which were delightfully decked out in a variety of Oldham Athletic memorabilia. Everywhere you went, people were talking about hardly anything else other than the game.

The Littlewoods store display with the cup

When the big day arrived it was the culmination, for me, of a lifetime of watching Oldham Athletic. I had witnessed all the things written about in my introduction and had experienced almost every football emotion possible. In effect, I had been waiting a long time for this 'something special' to happen. My mate, Phil, had booked my trip to Wembley through a travel agent and he recollected that we paid about £80 for the overnight stay at a hotel near one of the airports; this included breakfast and coach travel. There were four of us in the party but only Phil and I had the big daft hats which we had first worn when we watched the 6-0 semi-final drubbing of West Ham. Time for an amusing anecdote.......

Amusing Anecdote 14: Phil had a big surprise for us as we left C&A's on the coach for our Saturday journey to our London hotel. He had been secretly working on a banner that we were going to display in the Wembley stands. It was quite big and displayed the words 'Ooh! Roger Palmer,' a common cry among the Latics fans. He was very proud of his accomplishment and he slowly unfurled the banner to completely amaze us as he fanfared his nimble dexterity with cotton and thread. It was one of those magic moments that every practical joker hopes for and I was the opportunist who was ready to take full advantage. I casually remarked, *"Phil, there's no 'D' in Roger!"* He gave me one of those looks that said, 'You're taking the Mick,' and then realisation set in! Suffice to say, Phil spent his Saturday night, after finding an accommodating lady to lend him a needle and cotton, removing the letter D and moving the G,E and R down to fill in the space. We were in the bar getting tanked! You couldn't make it up!

The banner with a top hat obscuring the offending D

Ticket at the ready

We're on our way to Wembley

"We are the Boys in Blue... ooooh.. ooooh.... ooooh"

The big day finally arrived and after breakfast we boarded the coach and set off for the famous twin towers. The trip was very memorable and everyone was in very high spirits. The coach had a small TV screen at the front and a radio/stereo system. The driver was constantly replaying *'The Boys in Blue'* which was a special cup final song which was recorded by the team along with Cannon and Ball, the local comedy due who were also Oldham fans. The supporters really got into the spirit and almost everyone on the coach was singing along at the tops of their voices – it was a special memory.

When we finally arrived at the stadium, I can't remember if we went into a pub or not but I remember that we were drinking so maybe we had taken along some cans. The game became known as the friendly final due to both sets of supporters being so well behaved and mutually respectful of each other. I'll never forget the scene on Wembley Way with hoards of opposing supporters mixing together and having their pictures taken with their arms respectfully around each other. It's what football should be like.

Phil takes up the story, *"We were sat to the right at the top of Wembley way and were watching the two sets of supporters come round the corner and up towards us. When we saw they were Forest fans we kept quiet but when the Latics supporters came round we held the banner up high and started singing Oo! Roger Palmer (spelled correctly by then) which every one, to a man, responded with the same chant back. It was fantastic, the best feeling ever is the bond between true supporters."*

Both teams were entering the game on a downer as Forest had only won one game in ten and Oldham had only won one in sixteen (on grass). Joe Royle said before the game, *"They are a talented side full of internationals who are managed by probably the best manager in the game. It won't be easy for Oldham but we'll just carry on playing as we have been doing all season. We'll pay due respect to them and will try to do what we are good at: playing football; hustling; not giving them time to play their game; we'll try to get wide; we'll try to get crosses in; we'll try to entertain; we'll see what happens."*

When Brian Clough and Joe Royle walked their teams out onto the pitch they did so as the two longest serving managers in the entire Football League; the pair could easily have been likened to the 'Pauper and the Prince,' and that's not being disrespectful to Joe. It was a proud moment for everyone on the field and I also felt the pride build up inside, in addition to the anticipation of that 'something special' going to happen again. We were the famous Oldham so we couldn't lose, could we? I know that Rick has never watched the game on video and he has left the match report to me but..... all I can report is that Nottingham Forest won the game with a single goal from Nigel Jemson. The match, for me, was a nonentity and I don't know where the time went to as the game seemed over just after it started. I remember my mate, Phil, walking down towards the field and throwing his top hat onto the field at the end of the game. I instinctively did the same in a trance-like symbolic gesture that it was all over.

The trip back was a total contrast to the trip to the stadium. Fans were subdued, tired and physically and mentally exhausted. The coach driver put on a video to help drown the sorrows but it was a kind of horror-type soft-porn tape; the main dialogue being, "It's a sign..." which was the trigger for the actors to shed their kits and start doing rude things. It was pathetic really but we needed something to laugh at. All the after match reports were very complimentary to the Latics team but the game will be remembered mostly for the interaction of the supporters of both teams who fully played their part in the day.

Ian St John later raved about the performance of Oldham and said that there had been no way of distinguishing which team was the Second Division outfit as they were in no way inferior to their conterparts. The team had come back with their heads held high in the knowledge that they had done the town proud after a magnificent cup run that would live on forever in the hearts of the priviledged who were lucky enough to be there to witness it. 'Big Joe' declared, *"No way have we disgraced ourselves, in fact I'm very proud. We've had a fantastic season, it's been a lovely adventure – unfortunately the fairy tale hasn't come true today... but there's still time."* His counterpart, Brian Clough, admitted, *"They scared me to death... they never stopped coming at us from the first moment until the last."* Andy

Ritchie added, *"At least we've given a bit of a weekend for the fans, which is all that metters to us. We've got ambitions, but the fans are the ones who pay our wages, and if we've given them a good time then we're pleased about that."*

All pals together - fans mingled before the friendly final

The sea of blue lap up the atmosphere

The bottom line is that both clubs and sets of fans did the country proud. Of the 74,000 fans at the match only fifteen were arrested, of which six were from Oldham – the arrests were mainly drink related. The Oldham fans had waited around 90 years for it and I think that the players were moved by the reception they received as they entered the field. They came out of the game with credit and dignity although the pain showed through on the player's faces at the final whistle, but they had given their all and nobody could ask for more. It was still Oldham's day whatever the outcome. Tens of thousands turned out for the open top bus ride to a civic reception which was ended with a message from Rick Holden who promised, *"We're going to get promotion for you."*

Amusing Anecdote 15: Nottingham Forest's Franz Carr's relationship with manager Clough turned a bit sour after Clough locked him in the City Ground boiler room. Cloughie considered that Carr had put in a particularly dire performance against Athletic in the cup final and decided to take the unusual step as punishment. He always was a bit different was Cloughie, but that's what made him so special and respected.

Oldham v Manchester United – FA Cup Semi Final 1994 1-1.

Sunday 10th April 1994
Wembley Stadium 3:00pm

OLDHAM		MANCHESTER UNITED
Jon Hallworth	1	Peter Schmeichel
Craig Fleming	2	Paul Parker
Chris Makin	3	Denis Irwin
Neil Pointon	4	Steve Bruce
Richard Jobson	5	Lee Sharpe
Mike Milligan	6	Gary Pallister
Nick Henry	7	Dion Dublin
Paul Bernard	8	Paul Ince
Rick Holden	9	Brian McClair
Graeme Sharp	10	Mark Hughes
Darren Beckford	11	Ryan Giggs
Andy Ritchie	12	Brian Robson
Neil Adams	14	Nicky Butt
Manager: Joe Royle		Manager: Alex Ferguson

Referee: Philip Don (Middlesex). Linesmen: Roy Pearson; Bill Jordan.

Crowd: 56,399

This was the first return to Wembley for Oldham as it also was for me. I have to say right from the beginning of this escapade that I did not agree with the fixture being played there, I still don't and I never will! Wembley is supposed to be, or was, the place of finals – not a money-making experience for the FA and a money-sapping experience for the fans. To me it totally devalues the competition! It's now getting more stupid because the FA want every major semi-final played at the new Wembley stadium to help re-coup the money that they wasted on it in the first place!

In 2011 the FA Cup semi-final draw included four northern-ish teams. Stoke drew Bolton and the Manchester teams were drawn against each other but where did they play the ties? Wembley! Why did they not play them both at Old Trafford and make the stadium 50/50 in terms of support so that it was in effect a neutral ground? Anyway, I was less than impressed with this Wembley decision rubbish, but we had no choice, so we had to play United at Wembley! Our opponents in the final were to be either Luton or Chelsea but as Chelsea had won their semi on the Saturday, it would have been them. We had seen them off twice in the league games, so we would have been confident and competent enough to give them a run for their money and win the FA Cup!

In the league we were doing fine and looking like we were going to survive. I had re-joined Oldham from Manchester City in October and we had started to pick up. I was undoubtedly in the form of my life and trying to keep a club that I felt so passionate about in the Premier League or whatever the jerks called it then – let's just say 'top flight football.' The build up to the game had created 'cup mania' again in Oldham and, once again, the fans went mad for it! I bloody knew it would come to grief because people were going overboard with the cup and I felt that I was the only one who had a sense of deja vu in the club. I knew that if we lost we would be in the shit and so right I was. But we shouldn't have lost. We dominated the game from start to finish and fu*kin' lost again.

The team wasn't as talented as the 1990 team and there is no argument with that, but it had as much character and grit and should have been successful. The previous season the team had shown this fire in the survival campaign which saw them beat Manchester United, Liverpool, Aston Villa and Southampton in the last few weeks of the campaign. These games will no doubt be in other players' and fans' top 14 games; they are not in mine simply because I was at Manchester City at the time and I was admiring them from afar!

Prior to the game we had been training down in Sale, where Willy Donachie lived, as he had managed to hire out Sale Hockey club which had vast areas of lovely bowling green standard grass which we could train on. Willy had marked out the exact dimensions of Wembley and we then were taught how to defend against Manchester United on this size of pitch! In our previous games against United we were never out-played but often out-thought or put it simply in footballing terms 'we had been done.' And we were always done on the break by their electric speed and ability to counter attack after absorbing pressure!

One particular game stands out when we played them in the first year back in the top flight at home. We took the game to them and had them under the cosh for long periods of time. Then, as quick as a flash they would absorb an attack and Schmeichal would throw the ball out to Giggs or Kanchelskis and they would rape us for a goal! Then we would claw our way back into the game only for the same sucker punch to happen again.

This was a mixture of bad defending and poor concentration! The poor defending started at the top of the field where the scenario would happen like this: they would throw the ball out to their fullback, let's say our old player Denis Irwin and I would close him down; he would play the ball to Roy Keane in midfield (inside right) and he would not be closed down by our midfield because we hadn't learned to press together or drop together; he would then play it back to the advancing Denis Irwin who had gone past me on momentum because I had got too tight and that created an overload situation with Kanchelskis against Andy Barlow! Hence they were in behind us due to one piece of mis-timed defending.

In the semi-final at Wembley, Willy had us all drop to the half way line so as not to get sucked in, but to defend from the half way line. It worked a treat and we frustrated United all game as well as dominating large tracts of play! It was of course a tight game because they were the best team in the land and getting better, and we were resurgent. I had the better of Denis on the day and really enjoyed the whole Wembley experience. I wasn't nervous or star struck and I was so confident that, in the warm up, I was doing some show-boating skills with control of long range passes with Craig Fleming in front of the United players. I could tell from the reaction of their players that they were less than amused by me controlling 50 yard passes on the outside of my foot and flicking the ball up on to my head before hitting half volley return passes to Norland (Craig). Yet again Wembley was hot, we had a huge and noisy following and our lot were every bit as loud as the United fans.

Parker and Holden tussle for the ball

Extra time was reached with ease but frustration. Craig Fleming bossed Mark Hughes all game long and Man United were very bogged down in their general play. I took a corner in the second period of extra time and put it in with real inswinging pace. Thanks to an enormous cock-up involving Bruce, Pallister and Schmeichal, when they all seemed to collide, Neil Pointon hooked the ball home. We were in charge and they were deflated.

Then the moment that changed our whole season occurred. No, not the Mark Hughes volley, but a missed near open-goal by Sharpy! I had won a free kick against Denis around the edge of the box and, sensing that they were all knackered, took a quick free kick and clipped it into the six yard area. With United at our mercy Sharpy hit his shot into the side netting. We would have obviously won if he had scored. They, buoyed by the miss, went down the other end and then disaster struck! Again it was a mistake, because we had actually won the ball back and it was in the 120th minute. Neil Pointon had the choice of passing the ball to me, whence I would have run Denis Irwin down into the corner because he was dead on his feet, and run the clock down. His other choice would be to have booted it into row Z – he chose row Z. It was a good decision but, because the referee added time on, it allowed them to take a throw in to give a chance to Hughes who scored an unbelievable volley which got them out of the shit. I think we all mentally died in the bath after the game as we knew we had lost a great chance to get to the FA Cup Final for the second time in four years.

It took the wind out of our sails and in the replay we were undone by their counter attacking style yet again! It was strange that Joe played me on the right in the replay and I think he will agree that he made a mistake in the first game by not making a couple of momentum breaking substitutions by putting Andy Ritchie or anyone else on. But we were done for, and it caused our relegation and confirmed my hatred of the distraction of cup football which continues to haunt clubs to this day. It was so sad that we had lost to United twice in two FA Cup semi-finals within four years. However, they were still great days in Oldham's history and the fans will remember them to the end of their days. Now I am going to cheer myself up by going back a few years to a truly great game in my opinion. After the game, I was confronted by a journalist outside the ground who asked me if I was disappointed with the result? *"No,"* I declared. *"I am delighted!"* The mind boggles!

The build up to the game had another fantastic effect on the town. Everyone was buzzing at what was the third attempt at reaching the FA Cup Final in the history of the club. Souveniers were being snapped up at the club shop at a rapid pace and supporters were busy orgainsing travel to the tie. Joe Royle was by now an established manager as he had been at Boundary Park for 12 years and had brought the club lots of success. As Rick explained we had always given a good account of ourselves against Manchester United but we always seemed to have been caught out by their cunning or maybe it was just our bad luck. The Monday before this match United had won the league game against Oldham at Old Trafford by a 3-2 scoreline. The fans were getting pretty sick of losing out to them, particularly when it was near the end of the game so it was hoped that this time we would 'do them' for a change. United were sitting pretty on top of the Premiership table while Athletic were languishing at the other end, just four places from the bottom.

The pre-match news from United was that Eric Cantona was suspended. The tie occurred on a windy day and in the first half Lee Sharp muscled down Neil Pointon by shoving him in the back, in the penalty box, but the appeal was turned down by the referee, much to the amazement of almost everyone in the stadium. Graeme Sharp had the best chance for Oldham and should have scored but his shot to the left of Schmeichel was well saved which left the half-time score at 0-0. In the second half it was Sharpe again who had the best chance but he had another good effort saved when the keeper got down sharply to his right to block the shot. This left the full-time score at 0-0 so Alex Ferguson's prediction of lots of goals did not come to fruition. Once again, the tired Oldham legs were asked to play out another extra time session – over the recent seasons they had become masters at playing extra time and I often wonder if they ever set any records for the most periods of extra time played!

United almost took the lead in the first period after Denis Irwin centred a ball onto the head of Mark Hughes who had his flying header well saved by Jon Hallworth who acrobatically tipped the ball over the crossbar. Half way through the second period, with the score still at stalemate, Andy Ritchie was getting ready to enter the field of play as a substitute. Rick Holden took a right wing corner which Schmeichel found much too hot to handle and he spilled it into the path of Neil Pointon who volleyed the ball past a bemused clutch of United defenders to put the Latics ahead in the 106th minute. Ritchie immediately put his track suit back on and sat down in the dugout. Butt came on for Parker in a desperate attempt to level the scores. Sharp could have scored another goal and when his attempt hit the side netting most of the stadium erupted as they thought it was 2-0. With one minute remaining and with United pushing everyone forward except their keeper, Mark Hughes scored a magnificent volley to level the scores. It could have gone anywhere as he was leaning backwards, but it flew past a stunned Hallworth to silence the Oldham faithful who had been so close to going to Wembely for their first evet FA Cup final. Even to this day, Oldham fans despise Hughes for scoring, as they call it, 'that goal!' The Latics fans continued to sing, *"We love you Oldham, we do"* but in truth, Oldham Athletic never recovered from that moment, just 60 seconds away from glory. They began a journey which was a downward spiral; it was only halted when they reached the third tier of English football, which is where they remain until this day.

The future could have been so different for Oldham had Hughes not thundered in one of his trademark volleys that rescued United and gave them another chance to book their place into the final against Chelsea. *"He's probably never left it that late before,"* uttered commentator John Motson immediately after the equaliser. Oldham fans are still haunted to this day by the feat, such things can make or break clubs and in Oldham's case it broke them! It broke their team spirit, morale, belief and just as important their finances. These hugely affect matters on the pitch as well as off and Oldham Athletic fell apart. I'll leave it to the Oldham fans to have the final say.......

One fan recalled, *"I had just lit my celebratory Benson & Hedges when Mark Hughes mis-cued and scored the equaliser. The extra long tube journey back to Central London had to be endured to the strains of, 'You thought you had won... You were wrong.' We knew in our hearts that our one and only chance had gone. I gave up fags for ever the following October."*

Another fan said, *"We stayed at a hotel in Beaconsfield the night before the semi. As we were checking in, the Chelsea team were gathered in the foye for details about their trip to Wembley for their own semi-final. I had a good chat with Dennis Wise and Tony Cascarino and was very surprised to hear how much they knew about our players. It ended with them wishing us all the best and hoping to see us in the final."*

Barry Noble recollected, *"I didn't go to the Wembley game as I couldn't get the time off work. The manager was a Latics fan as well as me and I reckon he thought 'If I'm not going your not.' I was reconciled to watching the game at home on TV, dressed in my Oldham kit, but obviously not my boots! As I was working nights, I had to toddle off to work after the game so I didn't even have a consolation drink. I did manage to get to the Maine Road replay though with my wife and daughter. I drove down and parked on a side road, as you do. After the game we left the ground and went a different way to our car and we couldn't find it, so we had to retrace all our steps and go back to the ground and start from there. On the way back to the ground we passed loads of Manchester United fans and we were quite surprised that a lot of them wished us bad luck for the rest of the season. We managed to get a few hard luck and best wishes but mainly it was loads of grief."*

Another supporter laughed about his trip to the replay, *"I remember getting the coach down to Maine Road and our coach set off just at the same time as the team coach. Our quick-minded driver fell in right behind the team and we were escorted to the ground by a police escourt. We went through all the red lights in record time and I couldn't stop laughing all the way."*

Amusing Anecdote 16: Phil Stevenson tells, *"That day I actually thought we were going to beat the red bastards. It seemed to me that, at that particular time, we had the best team I'd ever seen at Boundary Park. Obviously I was really 'up for the cup' that day, as we all were from the Elevenways pub. As usual I sorted almost all of the trip out. On the day of the game we were to meet in the pub from 8:30am onwards. I arrived at about 8:15am, only to set a good example you understand, but* guess who was there before me? Yep, it was Eric (one of the regulars), who was only on his third pint!

I had instructed everyone that they should bring some alcohol to drink on the way down to Wembley because we only had time to stop once at some services about half way. Fu**ing hell! the coach was almost over loaded with the stuff. Two litre bottles of gin, two litre bottles of rum, alcops, packs of lagers, Guinness, half bottles of whiskey and brandy. We left the pub about 10:30am and everyone was well oiled by then. I think there was about 12 or 14 of us on board with a few 16 and 17 year old girls. Most of us had had four or five pints before we set off and were dying for a pee by the time we reached the M6. Of course you can't stop on the motorway so Bainsey (another of the regulars) came up with the great idea of, 'If we sup the two litre bottles quickly we could pee in them and dispose of the bottles when we stop at the services.' Eric thought this was the best idea Bainsey had ever come up with, and immediately started to drink anything whether it was in a two litter bottle or not, proclaiming that every little bit helps.

We pulled into services just through Birmingham with everyone screaming for a pee (we had filled all of the bottles while the young girls had openly watched us). I was discussing with the driver about how long we had to stay as we pulled into the car park. The mini coach had two rear doors, like the old fashioned Transits vans, and I went round to the back doors to open them. As I opened them, Eric fell out and cut his head open on the tarmac. He then got to to his feet and said, 'Oh fu*k, pissed again.'

We arrived at the ground and pulled into the Wembley car park with very few other coaches there and decided we should head straight into the ground and savour the atmosphere with a beer or to two, which we did. The Latics fans were superb, as they always are for big games and especially so against the scum (our affectionate name for Manchester United). The game or the result doesn't need reliving but on the way out I got man-handled but not actually hit by some United fans, and in the scuffle they knocked off my home made FA Cup trophy hat (it was quite large) and then stamped on it – bastards!

I'd had a couple of pints at half time and by the time I came out of the ground I had no idea at all which direction the coach was, or for that matter what it looked like. I decided to make my way over to one of the many exits where the coaches were leaving, looking and hoping if I could get lucky. A good half hour had past and I thought to myself, 'I'm hitching it home! I looked in my wallet – £5. That's it I thought, I'll ring my wife and tell her I'll be home late. I then heard, 'You fat fu**er, we're all waiting for you. Come on, the coach is over here.' It was Eric. Ah! happy days."

Oldham v Chelsea – First Division
1991/92 3-0.

Wednesday 21st August 1991
Boundary Park 7:30pm

OLDHAM		CHELSEA
Jon Hallworth	1	Dave Beasant
Gunnar Halle	2	Steve Clarke
Glynn Snodin	3	Tommy Boyd
Nick Henry	4	Andy Townsend
Earl Barrett	5	Paul Elliott
Richard Jobson	6	Kenny Monkou
Neil Adams	7	Graham Le Saux
Ian Marshall	8	Alan Dickens
Graeme Sharp	9	Kerry Dixon
Mike Milligan	10	Frank Sinclair
Rick Holden	11	Dennis Wise
David Currie	12	Joe Allon
Paul Kane	14	Kevin Wilson
Manager: Joe Royle		Manager: Ian Porterfield

Referee: G Singh (Wolverhampton). Linesmen: G Cain
(Bootle); AM Davies (Wrexham).

Crowd: 14,997

This was one of my favourite games for Oldham for several reasons. Firstly, it was a massive thing for all of us associated with the club to fulfil our dream of bringing First Division football back to Boundary Park. The fans had waited a lifetime to watch consistent top flight footy in their own town and, as players, we were desperate to get our new status as a First Division club up and running. We especially wanted a win as we had gone down 2-1 at Liverpool in the first game of the season the Saturday before; it was a game that we should have got at least a draw out of!

From a personal point of view I wanted to get back to top flight football. I was so up for this game and excited as it was my destiny game for Oldham. All I had dreamed of when I signed for Oldham in the Second Division was to play top level football in England for Oldham Athletic. If I had told anyone when I signed for Oldham that that was my goal they would have said that I was mad.

Why did I have such ridiculous aspirations of little Oldham competing and beating all the other big teams in the Second Division (now the Championship)? Teams like Sheffield Wednesday, West Brom, Middlesbrough, West Ham, Leicester, Portsmouth, Wolves, Newcastle, Blackburn, Ipswich and Bristol City, who were all undoubtedly bigger clubs than Oldham, and yet I had the belief that we would beat them all and get to the promised land! Once I had fulfilled my dream, what right did I have thinking that I was going to dominate teams visiting Oldham, like Chelsea, on that night? It was my destiny in short. I knew that I could play at that level since I was a kid but it is one thing thinking it and another thing doing it!

On the day of the game I was so emotional and fired up that I didn't get much sleep in my usual routine which was: bed the night before at 1:00am, after a huge meal and a Clint Eastwood film, or a few Laurel and Hardy short films; then up at 9:00am to run Jean to work! I often bought a newspaper, the *Today,* which is now sadly defunct and then it was back to bed. I would drift off until lunch time and then get up at 12:30pm and wander down to 'Bizzy Lizzie's' fish and chip shop (the best in the land) to get fish, chips and mushy peas and a couple of baps (bread rolls for the uninitiated). Then it was back to bed for some more zeds and up again at 4:30pm for a huge mug of sweet tea and toast before high tailing it down the road to the ground for the kick off.

Evening games were just the ticket for me as they allowed maximum rest and maxi fuelling to make sure that I was in tip top condition before the game. I had to be because my position as a winger probably demanded more energy expenditure than any other position on the pitch (and it is proved so don't get on your high horse!) so it was important that I got the prep right! Before I drove to the ground I had usually been for a brief walk up Embsay Crag, my spiritual mountain, to make myself feel better. I had, since a boy, felt that I was a mountain lad from the dales – in short – a fell runner, and I thought that it was where I was made. It is the toughest sport in the world and great grounding for professional football.

Imagine running up mountains and then tumbling down them at all costs. It is awesome as a spectacle and puts the fear of God into ordinary punters, but it is the domain of world class athletes and they go on to great, great things. Fred Reeves and Kenny Stuart were, and still are, world class athletes whose records fail to be matched, let alone beaten today – this is some 30 years later when they set them! Kenny Stuart, from Sedburgh in Cumbria, came second in the 1989 Houston marathon with a time of 2hrs 11mins! How mint was that? The whole world semed to turn up to the event and got sprinted out of it by Kenny Stuart, and that is class my friends.

Anyway, I digress from my point which is that it is so important to get yourself in tip top shape before a game and I did just that. Apart from the fell running I had another advantage in pro-footy, in that I had played rugby union which really does toughen you up! So, I was in all respects ready for Chelsea, and that Wednesday night was my time in football! My goal is out there somewhere on the World Wide Web for all to see and I can't find it, but it arrived, and it was my greatest moment for Oldham Athletic. The atmosphere was electric on that barmy August summer evening as our expectant crowd crammed the stadium in the hope for a winning start back home. It was also our first game back at home since May when we had won the Second Division Championship with the last kick of the season by Neil Redfearn – the penalty which turned all the lads into winners at last! The crowd for the evening was later reported to be 14,997 but we knew, as players, that there wasn't an empty space left in the ground for this historic evening and recorded figure must have been another one of Alan Hardy's accidental miscalculations to confuse the tax man. As if! Back in those days we were packing the stadium as our loyal Latics fans turned up in their thousands, and some of the figures released on the PA system were laughable.

In the first few minutes we were all over Chelsea and I know that they suddenly realised they were on a hiding to nothing. Joe was worried about how we would react following our great display at Anfield on the Saturday, only to get nothing, but he needn't have worried. The beauty of having a mid-week game after a Saturday defeat is that you don't have long to dwell on the defeat and can quickly get it out of your system. The opposite, of course, is losing a game prior to a lay-off such as International matches, because it takes ages for the next game to come around. We were back home now and nothing was going to stop us winning. We were so confident in the dressing room and during the warm up.

We had turned Boundary Park into a fortress and it didn't matter that we were back on grass. The place invoked fear into the opposition. The crowd, particularly in the Chaddy End, made enough noise for 20,000 and was our 12th man, whereas the weather was often our 13th man. In the first few minutes I was fouled by Dennis Wise and he tried to do one of those apologetic, 'sorry matey tap on the head gestures,' but I just brushed him off and took a quick free kick. I wasn't in the mood for friendly banter and jocundity!

My goal chance came; the ball was played over the top behind the fullback, Steve Clarke, and I raced on to it. It took a touch off my foot and it sat up for me to hit a sweetly timed half-volley which flew into the net, half way up at the near post giving Beasant no chance. I had to hit it early as Clarke was bearing down on me and had a chance of a block. Lift off! The crowd went bananas and so did I. I wheeled away towards the Chaddy End to receive their adulation. There was such a buzz and Chelsea were now being run ragged. This, to me, was where we should have been at, back playing top flight league football against massive clubs with big crowds.

Rick Holden's first goal - a fantastic feeling to score an Oldham goal at home in the top flight

Cup football has its own charm and it is unique for many reasons, but it was never in my opinion as good as playing consistent top league football. Cup runs give you confidence to be able to take form into the week-in week-out fight for league success and we were putting that into action. All the big teams that we had beaten or pushed right to the edge were now going to taste what it was like playing Oldham on a regular basis. We were to also find out what it was like and so this game against Chelsea, for me, was back to the start!

My second goal came in the 41st minute and killed Chelsea as they were already two down. Earlier in the half Marshy raced through on to a ball played by Bert and as he bore down on the goal he blew Elliott away in his wake and blasted a volley past Beasant who seemed to shy out of the path of the ball when you look at the picture. It was a tremendous strike and equal to mine in ferocity. 1-0 and on our way but my goal put further distance between us at 2-0, but you just never know.

In the dressing room at half time we talked about the need to avoid giving Chelsea a life line with our loss of concentration, and that the best way to do this was to keep attacking them. Joe kept emphasising this and we went out with a very positive attitude as we knew, as you all do, that at 2-0 you are never safe. 2-0 can very quickly become 2-1 (which is stating the bleeding obvious) but when it happens it can make you jittery and nervous and it is easy to throw away a 2-0 lead. 3-0 is a bigger and more daunting task for the trailing team and we put the game beyond doubt when David Currie clipped a ball into the top corner after a superb bit of skill, towards the end of the game to finish off Chelsea.

The Londoners were anaemic on the whole, posed little threat and meekly laid down at Boundary Park like so many big teams had done over the last couple of seasons. To me, this was just what I wanted. It put a message out to the rest of the country that we were in business against big clubs in league football, as well as cup football, and we were to be feared. The cup success in short was not a flash in the pan. It was serious stuff. From this game I knew we would survive. David Currie was known as Doddy, and was a superb player in my opinion. He loved running at defenders and was a highly skilled and talented player. He was last in and first out at training but he was a well-liked personality in the dressing room. He got his nickname from Neil Redfearn who likened him to the famous English comedian. Redders would often peel an orange and turn it inside out and cut slits in it to create teeth and insert it in his upper gum and sit in the dressing room and talk to Dave. Cruel but hilarious, but 'Doddy' took it well and never said anything. That was what the dressing room was like and you had to be tough with a phlegmatic sense of humour.

The substitution of Glynn Snodin, our left back for a striker, Doddy, showed Joe's mentality. He wanted to score another goal whereas many managers would have taken a forward off and put another defender on to try to preserve a 2-0 lead. It was the versatility of Ian Marshall, who he dropped back into centre half from centre forward, that allowed him to do this, and had we conceded he would no doubt have thrown Marshy back up front and use three strikers to try to score another goal!

I cannot recall anything of particular amusement as a singular incident during before or after the game apart from Redders patting Dennis Wise on his head like a dog when Wise was fouled (makes a change), and on his knees. Wise didn't like that one bit but he was welcome to take Redders on at banter, there would be only one winner! What does stand out in my mind was the whole occasion and the atmosphere inside the stadium. I always preferred evening games, not only because it allowed me the best preparation but there was the buzz of night games.

The darkness outside the stadium made the light and the events inside seem all the more close and intimate. It may be false but I always got the impression that the fans made more noise at night than during the day games. Is this some trick of physics, like there is less background noise, or that the fans are just up for it? Maybe the fans enjoy night games because they have had all day at work to get ready to build up to it, and can't wait to go and let off some steam! Whatever the pervading reasons I do know that Chelsea were caught up in a maelstrom and couldn't cope. Rabbits in the headlights doesn't even begin to sum up our superiority. We were up and running no doubt about that.

This was another big match in the history of Oldham Athletic Football Club. The club were back in the big time after an absence of 68 years! The trip to Anfield just a few days earlier had been disappointing for the fans but the experience of being involved with it was absolutely incredible. We were rubbing shoulders with the elite – in fact we were the elite! 'Big Joe' had pledged that he would not be abandoning his go-for-goal policy that had brought such substantial rewards. He said, *"It's the only way for us to play. Taking chances got us through to Wembley against some big-name clubs. We have to be prepared to gamble again now that we are meeting them on a regular basis. I have no doubts that the players we have can adjust and do well. It will be a tough season, but we are ready for it."*

Things had changed at Boundary Park too. Gone was the artificial pitch which had served the club so well; the Chaddy End had been made all-seater (much to the displeasure of many of the regular supporters); a hospitality suite had been erected; and the Latique Club shop had re-opened and was doing a brisk trade in the now First Division merchandise. The club had splashed out £1.6m on new players which seemed like chicken feed to their counterparts, however the club planned to live within their means. Within the last nine years the club had gone from being almost bankrupt to having an increased band of enthusiastic supporters, a successful team in the highest rank of football in England, a first class stadium, sponsorship and advertising, and a stability which would stand them in good stead which must be the ideal foundation to build upon.

Chairman Ian Stott was taking the accolades in his stride. he said, *"Gaining promotion to the First Division is the most important thing which has happened to this club in modern times. It is something we have worked for and dreamed about since I became chairman eight-and-a half years ago. The people who said we didn't want promotion were talking tommyrot. Far from not being able to afford to be in the First Division, we cannot afford NOT to be in the First Division. This is the start, rather than the end, of a new era in the history of Oldham Athletic Football Club."*

The pre-match programme notes from Joe Royle wrote, *"There have been many changes during the summer, both off and on the pitch, in preparation for our arrival amongst the elite of British football. A warm welcome to Graeme Sharp, Brian Kilcline, Craig Fleming, Glynn Snodin and of course Mike Milligan (new players – Millie returning). Our pre-season preparation has gone very well, with eight victories out of nine matches. The day that we're often accused of not wanting has arrived. Tonight sees the Latics in the toughest league in the world. Whatever happens this season, we must enjoy the experience, players and supporters alike. As always your encouragement is all important, so please be patient and enjoy the realisation of a dream."*

The day's match programme included an Athletic v Newcastle United replica football programme from 10th September 1910, the corresponding first home match in the First Division after playing out a 1-1 draw at Aston Villa.

Front page of the replica programme

OLDHAM ATHLETIC
(Blue and White).

1
M'DONALD
Goal

2
HODSON
Right Back

3
HAMILTON
Left Back

4
FAY
Right Half

5
DOWNIE
Centre Half

6
WILSON (D.)
Left Half

7
BROAD
Outside Right

8
M'TAVISH
Inside Right

9
TOWARD
Centre

10
MONTGOMERY
Inside Left

11
DONNACHIE
Outside Left

Kick-off 3-30.

Referee : T. ROBERTSON.

Linesmen : { H. HARTLEY.
{ L. HITCHEN.

12
RIDLEY
Outside Left

13
RANDALL
Inside Left

14
SHEPHERD
Centre

15
STEWART
Inside Right

16
RUTHERFORD
Outside Right

17
M'WILLIAM
Left Half

18
LOW
Centre Half

19
VEITCH
Right Half

20
WHITSON
Left Back

21
M'CRACKEN
Right Back

22
LAWRENCE
Goal

NEWCASTLE UNITED
(Black and White).

Team sheets from the 1910 programme

The replica programme contained quite a nostalgic collection of advertisements which brought back many memories for me and I am sure many of the older supporters. They included: Oldham Massage, 2 Park Road; Swan Vestas matches; Butterfield & Tattersall, The Dental Surgery, 6 King Street; CC Mills, Hatter and Outfitter; Fletcher, Travis & Co Ltd, noted ales and stouts at the Old Grey Mare; D Gore, Raleigh bikes, 295 Oldham Road; Stanton's Travels, 112 Union Street; Ellison & Spark, Drapers & Outfitters, 13 Curzon Street; Latic's Cigar (2d & 3d each) at the Featherstall & Junction Hotel; Adam Lee, Coalman, Wellington Street; Kings Ltd, Football Goods, 61 Manchester Street; Cafe Monico, Union Street; Brown's Animated Pictures, Wallshaw Street; Friendship Hotel, Mumps; WM Taylor, Eyesight Specialist, 32 Manchester Street; Owbridge's Lung Tonic; S Makin & Sons, House Furnishers, 8 Bottom o' th' Moor; Albert Pearson, Photographer, 107 Manchester Street; Palace Theatre, Oldham; Empire Theatre, Oldham; Hippodrome Theatre, Oldham; Oldham Evening Chronicle; and the Sunday Chronicle which was available for purchase at 1d. Many of these products and businesses are long gone but I find these little snippets to be a fascinating look back at the cultural history of the town before the First World War. It makes me wonder just what it would be like to compare walking to the ground in 1910 to what it was like going to watch the Latics play Chelsea on that particular day. Oh for a time machine, it would certainly be interesting.

As Rick described the match so eloquently I will skip my match report, suffice to say that the experience was one of those never to be missed occasions. The night was electric and I fully agree with Rick that the stadium takes on a different aura when the floodlights are on. That particular night was so satisfying to send the mighty Chelsea Pensioners home to the capital with their tails between their legs.

Following the game Joe Royle said, *"It would have been quite possible to go to Anfield and take a hiding. Liverpool can do that to anybody. If we had lost there and gone into last night's game with dented confidence we could have been looking at a dodgy start to the season. As it is, we performed well at Anfield and maintained that form against Chelsea. It was a great atmosphere last night and great to pick up our first three points."*

Oldham v Notts County – First Division 1991/92 4-3.

Saturday 14th March 1992
Boundary Park 3:00pm

OLDHAM		NOTTS COUNTY
Jon Hallworth	1	Steve Cherry
Craig Fleming	2	Charlie Palmer
Andy Barlow	3	Richard Dryden
Nick Henry	4	Chris Short
Richard Jobson	5	John McClelland
Ian Marshall	6	Mark Draper
Neil Adams	7	Andy Williams
Andy Ritchie	8	Phil Turner
Graeme Sharp	9	Gary Lund
Mike Milligan	10	Kevin Bartlett
Rick Holden	11	Dean Yates
Roger Palmer	12	Steve Slawson
Paul Bernard	14	Paul Harding
Manager: Joe Royle		Manager: Neil Warnock

Referee: KJ Breen (Liverpool). Linesmen: AJ Hill (Little Bispham); GJ Wilkinson (Preston).

Crowd: 12,125

We knew that this was a 'must win' game because we were sliding towards the relegation zone and we had lost the last four games: Aston Villa (A) 1-0; Wimbledon (H) 0-1; Everton 2-1; and Arsenal 2-1. We just had to win this game and I sensed that if we did it, it would ensure survival, both in points and in our psychology! We hadn't been playing badly but we were not winning, which is obviously the key to football and almost doesn't need saying. The reality being that three of the four clubs we had recently lost to were, and still are, giants of the game so there was no shame in losing to them. One team was a phenomenon and, though it had bad times, is still in existence and resurgent again, albeit as a new team. But that didn't help matters as we were in dire times and desperately needed a win.

We started nervously against Warnock's County, who were the helpers of our dramatic championship win earlier in the year by beating West Ham and thereby securing themselves a promotion play-off match. They won their play-offs and thus ensured England's oldest club a place back in the First Division. For this reason we knew they were tough cookies, and I feared them. On a personal note I also had issues with them. Their full back, Charlie Palmer had consistently been at me and we had, in the past, some very physical encounters. He had elbowed me off the ball many times until I eventually saw red and chased him down the field whilst play was going on at the other side of the pitch. That occurred the previous year and he didn't trouble me on this particular day. Incidentally, Joe had received some complaints from Latics' fans about my behaviour, after my chasing and volleying Palmer in the said incident. They had missed the abuse that I was getting, as did the referee. He then knew not to elbow me off the ball again!

County scored first in a clever move and it silenced Boundary Park. I thought we were going to struggle, especially as they had Bartlett running at us on the break and proving to be a menace! Earl Barrett had been flogged to Aston Villa in the February and he had always managed Bartlett very capably, but in his absence we were having problems. We pushed and shoved our way into dominance and then suddenly in the last ten minutes of the half we exploded into life and gave ourselves a lifeline. Marshy hit a superb diagonal into the area, described rather disparagingly by

Tony Bugby in the Oldham Chronicle as 'a long punt,' and Andy Ritchie (Stitch) rose superbly to head in on 38 minutes. It was a great goal and the timing was excellent.

We had missed Stitch through injury and his return made all the difference to our campaign of survival, which in essence it was! Four minutes later Stitch was at it again, this time a sublime finish after my corner was cleared. Marshy, again, was the provider of a neat through ball which Andy tucked away after a cute check back on to his left foot. On 44 minutes we won a corner, which I hammered, and it went into the top corner. These are flukes but are designed flukes if you understand. I had learned over the years, to hit balls from corners with such ferocity that they could cause consternation and might even go straight into the goal. It is rather like when you take an in-swinging free-kick and it goes in, but it is designed to if everyone misses it!

At 3-1 we would hope to be safe, but not us! We spooked ourselves by conceding a sloppy goal just after the break when former Leeds player Andy Williams spanked one into the top corner past Captain and then, with five minutes left, Lund got an equalizer with a header which Andy Barlow knows he should have dealt with. I was gutted but you never give up hope, especially with this Oldham side at the time, and we forced another corner which I whizzed in only to see it disappointingly cleared. Marshy had other ideas and raced on to it like an escaped baboon, and blasted it from 30 yards into the bottom corner to save the day. It was one of the best goals I have ever seen as he hit it on the rise and it went quail height at about 90 mph without looking like bouncing. That shot proved to me that he should have been playing for England. He was the best dual centre nod/centre half in the land, and him being overlooked by Graham Taylor, the England manager, was nothing short of criminal!

The sense of relief was amazing and did we celebrate? Damned right we did – we had 40 points and still had nine games to play so we knew that we were safe. We celebrated by going out and having a huge Chinese banquet, which got out of control and caused Joe another episode of fobbing the general public off on the Monday morning, but it was something that he had become good at; taking the rap for his cohorts and then bollocking us in an exasperated manner on the training ground at half-ten in the morning! *"Well Joe, you can't have it both ways. You sign a bunch of players who all have something wrong with them so what do you or did you expect?"* It was his creation!

This match was very important for the fans. They were getting used to the team playing in their new exalted place and certainly didn't want it to end. After the defeat at Highbury, the Latics were sat in 14th place in the league table with 37 points and a goal difference of -7. They had also played more games, Nottingham Forest had five games in hand, than every team trailing them, so nothing could be taken for granted.

Joe Royle was philosophical in his pre-match programme notes when he said, *"Closer examination of our defeats (last four games), would all reveal that we lost by the odd goal, three of them were away from home, and all three games should never have been lost. But there I go again using that word should! At Arsenal Jon Hallworth was not called upon to make a serious save in ninety minutes. I have steadfastly refused to speak to the press in London and Wednesday morning's tabloids confirmed my motives for ignoring them. It would appear that to be a headline writer, that you would need an IQ of no more than 20, no idea whatsoever of rhyming and a complete disregard for the truth. We now have nine games left to secure our First Division status, and your support is invaluable in making sure that our dream having been realised, is jealously maintained."*

As Rick has done yet another sterling job of describing the match action I do not need to add anything, suffice it to say that it was an incredibly important match to win and an exciting event to watch. You are never bored watching Oldham Athletic and that team, more than any, were amazing to support but they always had you on the edge of your seat. They had that never-say-die attitude to games and most match-ups had more twists and turns than the Hampton Court Palace's hedge maze. After the match the Latics had dropped to 15th place in the league table with 40 points and a goal difference of -6. So, although they had won, they had actually dropped a place by winning their last game! This is because other teams had been playing 'catch up' and every team below them, except for Luton Town who were level, still had games in hand on Oldham. It would still be a fight to survive.

Joe Royle described the win against Notts County as the 'most significant' of the season. He commented, *"In view of the opponents and the circumstances, I regard this as a most significant win. Yet I do not think we played as well as in some of the games we have lost of late."* There was unanimous praise for Marshy's winner from all and sundry, but Joe insisted, *"I still maintain though, that he is a centre half who can play centre forward."* How right he was too!

Notts County manager Neil Warnock gave praise to Oldham's Andy Ritchie by saying, *"He was the difference between the two teams. Ritchie is a good pro and right now I could do with a couple of players like him. We won the Second Division (by winning at West Ham) for Oldham last season and now we have probably kept them in the First Division this season."*

Oldham v Ipswich – Second Division 1990/91 2-1.

Saturday 27th April 1991
Portman Road 3:00pm

OLDHAM		IPSWICH
Jon Hallworth	1	Craig Forrest
Gunnar Halle	2	Frank Yallop
Andy Barlow	3	Neil Thompson
Nick Henry	4	Steve Palmer
Paul Warhurst	5	David Linighan
Richard Jobson	6	Brian Gayle
Neil Adams	7	Scott Houghton
Earl Barratt	8	Paul Goddard
Ian Marshall	9	Simon Milton
David Currie	10	Romeo Zondervan
Rick Holden	11	Chris Kiwomya
Neil Redfearn	12	Tony Humes
Paul Kane	14	David Gregory
Manager: Joe Royle		Manager: John Lyall

Referee: G Willard (Worthing). Linesmen: G Butland; D Madgwick.

Crowd: 12,332

This is undoubtedly the game which changed Oldham Athletic's history and the personal fortunes of all our players. We had to win this game to become winners. We may have captured the imagination of the nation and the hearts of the football fans to such an extent that we were everybody's second team but we were still losers, in my opinion anyway! Today was the day that we had the chance to put it right and become real winners. Win at Ipswich and we were guaranteed promotion to the top flight of football.

We had a photo shoot before the game and I am pictured sporting a beard which I had said that I was going to keep until we got promotion, and it looked ridiculous because it was ginger and I had black hair. But we were so focussed that we knew we were going to beat Ipswich! John Lyall, the Ipswich manager knew this too. He spent 90% of his programme notes praising us and what a lovely man he was also. A genuine football man who led Ipswich to success the following year in getting them promoted to the Premier League. I know he copied our model and he got Ipswich to the 'Promised Land.'

We travelled down the night before and it was business as usual, in that the management did their normal Friday night routine of going out on the piss (something we did at Barnsley several years later and now I know why); whereas we had to stay in and suffer the long slow night. I didn't sleep that well, and Captain was complaining that I was disturbing him by watching the television late into the night. He played his early career at Ipswich and was desperate to do well, but I wasn't making it easy. He always used to look after me by getting up early and letting me sleep in, and then bring me a coffee and toast at ten-thirty in the morning as well as a copy of the Daily Telegraph. He was, and still is, a giant rooster and enjoyed clucking about!

Unusually I had decided to have a little walk around the grounds of the hotel, which some managers insist upon but we were never pressured to do so at Oldham. I bumped into Joe and Willy Donachie doing the same. I encountered them and told them my thoughts. Joe asked me if I would repeat them to the lads in the dressing room before the game, which was rare and a bit daunting to say the least! Basically I said, and told the lads, that the day ahead, and thus I meant the game, was going to be the game that changed their lives forever and was the path to fame and fortune! They would become somebody and would make a fortune because of the way football was changing. But more than that they would become legends at Oldham Athletic and never have to worry about their status within the club! The speech seemed to go down well with the lads, and out we went onto the hallowed turf waiting for Ipswich fully revved up! In Andy Barlow's case, too revved!

In the first minute the ball got played out to Zondervan, their Dutch player (Ipswich liked signing Dutch players), and Andy launched him into the air and he landed on the top of the dugout, which at Portman Road was above the walkway between the stand and the pitch and quite high up! John Lyall was walking out to the pitch side smoking his customary cigar, and after the kick off he dropped his jaw like a jack hammer as Romeo flew through the air and landed on top of the dugout. That was welcome to the game if ever I saw it! Andy needless to say got booked but their danger man left the arena on a stretcher!

We more or less dominated them in a tepid game and once again Marshy proved to be the key player scoring two well taken goals, the second being a great header which sealed our promotion! They scored a late consolation but we were there in the big time and the celebrations began in earnest! There was a pitch invasion as the travelling faithful spilt on to the ground where we created our glory and hugged the players who were only too happy to return the greeting. Big Joe came up and gave me a bear hug and I felt relieved that I could at last shave my beard off. We played a good attacking controlled game with lots of width and I think that that team was as good as any in the last two years!

It was unusual to play Earl on the right of midfield but he was such an athlete and a truly great player in understanding the game that he could have played anywhere! Andy Ritchie was missing as was Roger Palmer but it didn't matter – we won and got promoted! The jubilation in the dressing room afterwards was unreal! We were spraying Champagne but I refused to do this. If you saw the British Masters Football in 2003 when

Manchester City won it, you will have noted that I was the only one drinking it and not spraying it, much to my mother's disgust! It went all over the place, and the genial Mr Lyall came in to congratulate us and he got drenched for his efforts! I can remember going round and grabbing each player by their face and wiggling their head in delight to tell him how proud I was of them in creating a dream come true, and only two years after I had signed for the club.

The cup glory was now, as I had said, insignificant as we had got to the place we wanted to be. Cups meant nothing now. This was glory and success. This was business, and we were now winners and a real threat to anybody's idea of an easy game. The bus journey home was an electric piss-up and I still recall bumping into Joe and Willy in an Indian restaurant later in the evening in Oldham and sharing a big hug! We did come down to Earth later as we were beaten by Notts County the following week; in the aftermath we had the biggest bollocking of the season by Joe! We were not world-beaters!

Amusing Anecdote 17: The amusing tale I remember after this game was about me having to shave my beard off because we won, which I duly did. We went out on our merry way back up north which took about four hours we landed back at Oldham around about 10pm. When we eventually reached the Oldham Mumps roundabout, there was a real old-fashioned nightclub, Disco X, and we decided to go in there. I later emerged and walked up Huddersfield Road towards a shop in Springhead named Garforth Glass. I walked past the window of an Indian Restaurant and saw Willie and Joe sitting there. I sneaked up and banged on the glass and it made a yug noise – you should have seen them leave their seats like Harrier jump jets. I got a bollocking for that one on the Monday too!

This was another massive day out for the fans, but by that time we were getting used to it and even cheekily starting to expect it! I was unfortunately away for this very important meeting so I will rely on my fellow supporters to examine the game and give their respected interpretions. After the incredible successes of last season and due to the limitations of the Boundary Park gate capacity, the club had introduced a new Latics Club Membership scheme for the beginning of the 1990/91 season. Supporters who signed up were issued with a Latics Club Member book which was almost identical to a Season Ticket book. The fans had to hand in a voucher, which was torn out of the book at the turnstile, for admission to the membership area. The club had approximately 5,000 season ticket holders and around 6,000 club members at the beginning of the season; as the season progressed so did the gates with regular attendances well above the 11,000 combined ticket holders.

Latics Club Member Book for 1991/92

An early season report by one fan described the season as, *"... the atmosphere is like being at Wembley every game. It really is unbelievable. We only missed the first game away and are hoping to go to Middlesbrough on Saturday but it may be too late for tickets as it is an all-ticket game and they have only allocated us 1,850. Without exaggerating, we took 5,500 to Barnsley the other week. Although we only drew 1-1 at home to bottom of the league Charlton we are still looking down on the rest of the Second Division. It's amazing!"* Even the part-time fans were coming out of the woodwork and were becoming 'regulars.' Exciting things were beginning to happen at the club once again.

Another supporter said, *"When we went to Ipswich, the day we went up, our driver got us there quicker than ever before. At 11:40am we were outside the ground wondering how long a wait we would have. We then went into the pub just outside the ground to be totally surprised to find a pub FULL of Latics fans chanting, 'We'll be up by 5 o'clock.' The atmosphere was just electric, time flew by and of course, we were up by 5 o'clock."*

Mick Cunningham reminisced, *"I remember that I was hugging random strangers on the terraces at Portman Road and I also spotted adopted Oldhamer Ken Riley sitting on a barrier looking completely stunned. On the coach trip back Queen was being repeatedly played and we all joined in singing, 'We are the Champions.'"*

Martin Bell recalled, *"Being at Ipswich when we got promotion was my best ever day as a Latics fan. I particularly remember some dark haired guy squeezing past us very politely in the stand. The next thing he was on the pitch shaking hands with Joe Royal, absolutely brilliant!"*

'Fryatt' told his tale, *"There were fourteen of us who set off at seven bells in the morning. We were in a mini-bus and we just flew across the country. We arrived at Portman Road and I fully expected us to be the first in the pub for the pre-match session. How wrong I was! It seemed we were late, and the place was just heaving with Latics' fans. I found out that the coach from the Candlelight Club had left Oldham at 2:00am in the morning, just after the club had closed! It was a lovely sunny day and nothing was stopping us. Ian Marshall had another of his great games and contributed with two finishes of supreme quality. After that it all seemed a bit of a blur.......... I do, however, remember getting back home in Oldham at about 2:30am after having plenty of stop-offs on route. Going up.... going up.... going up!"*

Joe Royle was beaming as he told the Daily Mirror, *"We'll make one or two landlords happy on the way home – it's nice to do it on grass – I'm very aware that people still put our success down to the plastic but we are looking forward to grass pitches in the First Division."* It was a definite go at the establishment as I feel that they were taking pleasure in telling Oldham that we had to rip up the plastic! I think it was quite appropriate that we got promoted away, playing on grass, just for the pleasure of shutting up any doubters.

Oldham v West Ham – League Cup Semi-Final 1989/90 6-0.

Wednesday 14th February 1990
Boundary Park 7:30pm

OLDHAM		WEST HAM
Jon Hallworth	1	Phil Parkes
Denis Irwin	2	Stewart Robson
Andy Barlow	3	Julian Dicks
Nick Henry	4	George Parris
Ian Marshall	5	Alvin Martin
Earl Barrett	6	Tony Gale
Neil Adams	7	Liam Brady
Andy Ritchie	8	Stuart Slater
Roger Palmer	9	Gary Strodder
Mike Milligan	10	David Kelly
Rick Holden	11	Kevin Keen
Scott McGarvey	12	Alan Devonshire
Willie Donachie	14	Tommy McQueen
Manager: Joe Royle		Manager: Lou Macari

Referee: L Shapter (Torquay). Linesmen: J Horswell (Repton); J Jones (Doncaster).

Crowd: 19,263

This was the most iconic game and still remains so in Oldham Athletic's history! Though I don't particularly like it, as you will have gathered from this book, I have to admit that it was one of our finest hours. West Ham, under Mr Lou Macari (whom I feel so sorry for in what happened in his personal life), were fish out of water on this evening. Unfortunately, history documents them making noises about how the plastic pitch wouldn't cause them any concerns, and how they would take a narrow defeat back to Upton Park and turn things around. They did turn things around but by then it was way too late! The game, being played on 14th February 1990, has become known as the St Valentine's Day Massacre and, but for Phil Parkes the West Ham veteran keeper, it would have been a double massacre as Parkes saved at least six certain goals, keeping the score down to just 6-0.

Prior to the game we were very confident that we could beat the Hammers but didn't quite expect the result we got, although my college buddy and lifelong friend, Melt, did. When we arrived in the car park Barry Davies, who along with John Motson were the main football commentators for most of the 70s, 80s and 90s on both channels of terrestrial television in England, asked me how we would do. Before I could answer, Melt said to him 6-0! Davies just opened his mouth wondering who this bloke was, and how he could come to such an outrageous conclusion. We didn't see him after the game!

It was obvious to us as a team that West Ham had come to defend and played five at the back which instantly led Joe Royle to push big Marshy up front and this immediately caused devastation. It was also clear that they had instructed their right back, Stuart Robson, to try to rough me up a bit, but his second foul on me after less than ten minutes saw him get the dreaded early caution which then rendered him useless for the rest of the game. They had an early attempt on goal but then that was it for the main. A bit of neat link up play from Marshy, Stitch and Bert resulted in a shooting opportunity from outside the box which Bert hit with his left foot from about 20 yards to give Parkes absolutely no chance. It was an instinctive effort on his weaker foot, but he was so good with his left that you could hardly call it that! We were never afraid to shoot and would practise taking shots early, particularly half-volleys which this was.

Willie Donachie used to set up sessions in training every day, more or less to practise the art which, on a surface as true as the plastic, made sense. The second goal on 19 minutes was similar, in that it again came from a longish range shot from outside the box. It was a case of 'out with the old and in with the new' as Nick Henry muscled the once brilliant, but now struggling for influence, Liam Brady off the ball to slip Andy Ritchie free to run at the opposition defence. They made the mistake of backing off and Stitch never needed any encouragement to shoot, which he did. Cruelly for big Phil Parkes, it took a deflection and wrong footed him and we were two nil up. I can remember thinking that this was too good to be true and was glad that we had at least something to take to Upton Park. For us to be in that position after only 20 minutes we knew we would have to avoid conceding anything from then on!

There was a stereotype, which was often overplayed and often not true, that southern teams didn't like Boundary Park because of their hostility to the weather. To call it inclement was a massive understatement and we did sense when teams 'didn't fancy it' when they played us. Often they would turn up in long sleeve shirts, gloves and tights, and that was just putty in our hands. When it started lashing it down we did get the sense that many, but not all, of the West Ham players would rather be somewhere else; when Earl forced my return cross, from a poor low corner, into the bottom corner to make 3-0 you could see them visibly wilt.

We could have had another goal when Marshy's header was brilliantly saved from another of my crosses. The Hammers were delighted to be in the dressing room at just 3-0 down when half time arrived. Half times are often crucial in footy and can come at the wrong time for some sides, so to speak!

We certainly didn't need it as we were so dominant and were scared that we might lose our momentum. We also thought that the 'Bleeding Hammers' might regroup and re-evaluate their thinking which was tactically too defensive. We feared that they would come out and snatch an odd goal which would give them hope for the remainder of the second half and for the return tie. Joe reminded us of their defensive frailties, which was out wide, and within a few seconds of the second half we got the goal that destroyed them. A typical triangle between Bert, Milly and Denis Irwin resulted in Den's cross which fell to me at the back post. I had practiced this a million times in training which was to assess the ball late. I watched it bounce and sure enough it kicked a little so I let it hit my chest and let it settle. At the right height I volleyed it into the corner of the net! When it went in they were shattered and the crowd went mad. I set off on a run towards the Looker's Stand and waited for the lads to catch up. We knew we were there now and, looking back, I can't help feeling what it must have been like for the poor West Ham players, management and supporters. Nobody really wants to see massacres and this was what was unfolding in front of them.

For the next 25 minutes there was a bit of a lull and they even scored, but it was ruled out for a foul. Then Roger Palmer got in on the act from a corner which Marshy flicked on from me. It was quite simple in its construction. Put the ball in with pace to one of three areas and the lads would do the rest. I never aimed for anyone – just areas with pace and made sure the keeper couldn't claim it. Anything dropping in the six yard box was usual prey to Rodge. The 'full house' crowd was dwindling, as many West Ham fans *'bubbles'* had long since faded away when Andy headed in a teaser from me after I when around Robson. He had completely gone by this stage and daren't tackle me. Again the construction was simple – beat your fullback – stand the ball up – watch centre forward run on and head in. Simples!

Andy and I were awarded the joint 'Man of the Match Award' but in truth it should have been Phil Parkes, even though he let six in. The dressing room was buzzing after the game but I quickly cleared off home and can remember overtaking the West Ham team bus on the motorway as they left town. It must have been heart breaking for them looking back now, but at the time there were not, as I can recall, any sentiments from us. We still had to finish the job at Upton Park and make sure we didn't have a nightmare. We subsequently did in losing 3-0 but we will never know how much of that was down to the fact that it was a non-event for us, and a pride thing for the Hammers under new management of Billy Bonds, who had replaced poor Macari who was sacked after the game. Cruel game it has to be said!

The joint 'man of the match' award

Amusing Anecdote 18: This event wasn't related to the game, but more the overall tie. It came to the surface after we had lost the return leg at West Ham 3-0 but we had still got to the final. A favourite haunt of ours was up at *The Black Ladd* public house, near to a place called Badger's Edge which was where Joe lived. His place was dangerously close to the pub but we were flying as we had achieved Wembley and didn't give a monkey's! The night roared on in the true Latics style of, 'If it's one out – it's all out!' The landlady was eventually persuaded to serve us topless, chiefly persuaded by the dark-horse himself. The next morning I slept in and forgot to pick up my future wife, Jean, at 11:00am from Manchester Piccadilly. Talk about 'down the banks and in the doghouse.'

I have expressed many times that this was one of my favourite all-time games in over fifty years of supporting Oldham Athletic. I made a vow as a young man that I would never go to Wembley unless it was to watch my team play there, and I honestly never expected that I would fulfil that wish as in the old days, Wembley was only the venue for cup finals and internationals. It therefore meant something special. I would even bring back the community singing. It still brings a lump to my throat when I hear *Abide With Me!* Today the new Wembley is used to host all types of 'mickey mouse' cups, shields, play-offs and various trophies that are available to all and sundry. Even non-league teams have the opportunity of playing on the 'hallowed turf,' as it used to be called. I do not begrudge these teams having the opportunity to display their wares on such a stage but only as it brings much needed revenue to semi-pro and grass-roots teams which can only be good for the game. However, I wanted my team to do it the proper way and this game was their best opportunity to rise to that success in 77 years when they had last appeared in a semi-final.

My 'holy' Oldham Athletic Club Card

The build up to the game was phenominal. Both teams were looking to be the first Second Division team to reach the League Cup final since 1981, a remarkable feat which was last achieved by none other than Athletic's visitors West Ham. The stage was set for a pulsating encounter with fans flurrying to get tickets for the game. Oldham had introduced a membership scheme at the start of the season whereby fans were given a card which was similar in design to a credit card. As the big games were played the fans would show their cards to get priority tickets and the club punched the card or cut a corner off so that it could not be used again – how 20th century! Such were the cup successes, combined with the numerous replays, that by the time I went for my West Ham tickets there was not much left of the card and it had more holes than a colander! Crowds were by this time phenomenal and sell-outs were almost a regular occurrence. The supporters even needed a membership card for the Clayton Arms pub which was situated at the back of the Chaddy End! I bet even those are a collectors item now, especially as the club decided, in their infinite wisdom, to bulldoze one of their best avenues of income.

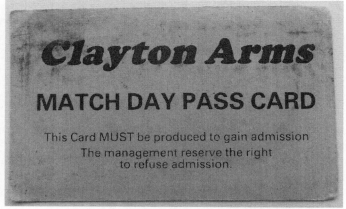

A pass was needed to have a pre-match pint!

Oldham had seen off Southampton in the quarter-finals after a 2-2 draw at the Dell and a 2-0 success at Boundary Park while West Ham's counterparts had been Derby County which they had dispatched 2-1 at the Boleyn Ground after a 0-0 draw at the Baseball Ground. Oldham had been unbeaten at home since January 1989 so the Hammers would have to come up with something extra special to break down the defence of one of the most successful home records in the League. The Latics entered the match as the bookies favourites to be journeying down Wembley way, but there was a two legged semi-final to get out of the way first before any celebrating could begin. The game was the Hammers second successive semi-final and their seventh in all.

On to the main business now. Paul Warhurst and Frankie Bunn were both injured and could not take part in the game and the news from the West Ham dressing room was that they had come with a game plan to use three centre backs to try to nullify the Athletic goal scoring machine. The kick-off had to be delayed by 15 minutes after hold ups in travelling and the shear physical effort required to get the volume of people into the ground.

The Latics kicked off attacking the Chaddy End and the first move of the game resulted in a free kick for the Latics after Stewart Robson cynically hacked down Rick Holden on the left wing just inside the West Ham half. A few minutes later Holden made a swashbuckling run down the left, beating three players, but his centre was headed away by Gary Stodder and it just missed the crossbar and landed on the roof of the net for an Oldham corner. The corner was knocked away by Kevin Keen for a second successive corner. It was a frenetic start and then Robson was booked for a second rash challenge on Holden. It was hard to imagine that it was still the second minute of the game as it had seemed like ages. In the 11th minute Neil Adams started a delightful move and passed the ball to Andy Ritchie who laid it back for Adams who hammered the ball with his left foot hard and low into the corner to make it 1-0 for the home side. It was a beauty!

Stuart Slater almost made an immediate reply for the Hammers. Straight from the restart he was put through on goal and it took an immaculate sliding tackle from Jon Hallworth just outside his box to clear the ball to safety after it had rebounded off Slater to end up on the roof of the net. Dennis Irwin was next to try his luck with a long range shot which went just wide. This was followed by another great cross from Holden which had 39-year-old Phil Parkes scrambling to make a good catch which he executed with perfection to thwart the danger.

In the 18th minute Ritchie intercepted a West Ham attack in his own half and set off running towards goal. The Hammers defenders parted like the Red Sea so Ritchie just kept going .... and going until he finished the run off by hammering the ball past Parkes to make it 2-0. The ball took a slight deflection en route but it wouldn't have made any difference to the outcome.

The goal maintained his record of scoring in every round of the competition and was his 23rd goal of the season.

Rain started to fall more heavily while Roger Palmer was foraging out on the right wing in the 23rd minute but he was unceremoniously brought to ground when he was hacked to bits by Julian Dicks. With just 13 minutes of the half left it proved to be very unlucky for West Ham as they went three goals down. Holden sent over a tantalising cross from the right wing which Palmer nodded down to Earl Barrett. Falling backwards, Barrett reacted quicker than the Hammer's defenders and bravely slid in and with his left foot to force the ball to the right of the despairing keeper. It was almost 4-0 minutes later when a great run from Adams on the left saw him lay the ball back for Holden who immediately centred the ball. Ian Marshall sent in a flying header which Parkes made a great save from. The save alone would have been worth the entrance money on the night. With the whole of the Oldham team playing to the peak of their form they went in at the half time whistle with a deserved 3-0 cushion to take into the second half while leaving West Ham a mountain to climb.

Oldham started the second half having scored 18 goals in their five home ties in this competition and it became 19 in the opening minute of the half after some great work on the right side of the field by Mike Milligan and Adams. The play resulted in Irwin centring the ball to Holden who was at the back of the box. Holden brought the ball down with his chest and hammered a left foot shot to the right of the keeper and the ball crept in perfectly, just inside the upright, giving the keeper no chance. It was Holden's seventh goal of the campaign and was the killer punch which almost guaranteed that the Latics would be the team making the esteemed trip to the twin towers as there didn't look to be any way back for the visitors. The game was turning into a rout!

Rick commented that he felt sorry for the visitors and that 'nobody really wants to see massacres.' Well I've got news for you Rick – the Oldham fans did! By this time they were baying for blood and were wondering just how many they could score, and I remember quizzically thinking if there were any more records to be broken (after the Frankie Bunn exhibition). I've always had a fascination with records, especially for my owm team. Alan Devonshire replaced Stodder in an attempt for West Ham to stop Oldham's scoring machine. At this stage of the game it was the Hammer's supporters who were singing in full voice. They repeatedly chanted, *"All we are saying is give us a goal!"* Robson did get the ball in the net but it was disallowed as the whistle had gone for a foul before the ball had even dropped.

The referee awarded an Oldham corner in the 70th minute, at which Tony Gale vehemently denied that it had touched him last. The resulting right wing corner was executed by Holden and leading goalscorer Palmer was on hand to slide the ball home with his left foot for the fifth goal of this pulsating game. Ritchie then splayed a pass out to Holden on the left wing. The winger beat his full back twice and, with lots of blue shirts waiting in the middle, then sent over a beautiful pin-point cross which Ritchie headed down and into the net to make a staggering record breaking 6-0 scoreline for the League Cup competition. The goal was number 24 of the season for the devastating striker and was his second of the game. The Oldham scoreboard went blank after the sixth goal – I think that it was totally overworked and just couldn't keep up with the swashbuckling, fearless, infectious and swaggering style of play that seemed to come straight out of an old time *Errol Flynn* pirate film.

Another left wing break came, this time from Nick Henry. If anyone on the night deserved a goal it was Henry who had bossed the midfield as if he had been taking a stroll in the park. However, he laid the ball back perfectly to Palmer and his attempt brought a scrambled save from Parkes after it had been kicked off the line by Dicks. The move deserved more rewards and a 7-0 scoreline would not have been out of place on the showing. Hallworth, one of the most under-rated keepers to have played at the highest level, had one of his easier nights and was never really troubled. The game finished at 6-0. Thousands of fans stormed onto the field at the conclusion to offer their congratulations on a result which was to always be remembered as the *'St Valentine's Day Massacre.'* It was a remarkable achievement and could anything stop Oldham now? As most pundits say in a home and away semi-final tie, 'It's only half-time!' but it was surely beyond the realms of possibility for the Latics to travel down to West Ham and lose by seven goals – or was it?

Amusing Anecdote 20: *"I was lucky (unlucky?) enough to be in the Caribbean in 1990, reporting on England's cricket tour. When we met West Ham in the first leg of the League Cup semi-final, England were playing (if memory serves) a one-day international. Anyway, what I remember clearly is attending a press conference the next morning and making sure I was in the front row while wearing my 'Andy Ritchie Appreciation Society' tee-shirt. England's captain, of course, was Graham Gooch – not only a top man but also a fanatical West Ham supporter. Goochy took it well – after initially feigning to walk out of the press conference on seeing my shirt. Four years later, I was back in the Caribbean for another England cricket tour. With me in the Barbados press box was Stuart Pyke, then working for IRN but best known to all Latics fans for his Piccadilly football reports. We shared an ecstatically happy few minutes when the 1994 FA Cup semi-final was 1-0 in our favour. What happened next we won't dwell on, except to say I never have seen that goal by the man whose named I cannot bear to utter, and I never will."* – David Lloyd (formerly cricket correspondent of the [London] Evening Standard).

An after match interview with manager Joe Royle revealed that he didn't expect anything like that and he said he would have been happy with a one or two goal win which would have been sufficient. He did admit that his side now looked like favourites but was cautious that there was still a professional job to be done. He was delighted that his team had unsettled the Hammers even though they had played with five at the back. His counter was to play with five up front and, although they caught us once or twice on the break, no real damage was done. The Latics had been relentlessly attacking and with just one central defender, Marshall was pushed forward to create havoc in the Hammer's defence, they had faced little challenge but what was achieved was done with a lot of style; there was an earthy, homespun charm to it all. It is rumoured that one fan even gave birth to twins during the game.

Joe's counterpart, Lou Macari, was quoted as saying, *"We were second best all night – the difference between the two sides was enormous, but I wouldn't criticise my players. If we had trained on that (the pitch) for three weeks it would have made no difference. They caught Arsenal and Southampton here as well; it was so one-sided it was unbelievable."* Well what else could he say? After this game the tills never stopped ringing in the Oldham club shop as souveniers were being snapped up in a conveyor belt type of frenzy as the fans couldn't get enough of anything related to Wembley. 'Big Joe' was later interviewed and asked what it felt like for the town, to which he responded, *"You have to live in the town to experience what it is like. The fans have been talking about going to Wembley ever since the Scarborough game so I know exactly what the fans are experiencing."*

Andy Ritchie confessed that he had been ribbed by the lads as they said that he should not have claimed his first goal as it took a deflection. Andy Barlow made him feel better whan he said, *"We will allow you the second goal as there was no doubt about it at all."* Ritchie was also very complimentary to the fans who had turned out in their thousands and had got behind the lads and supported them with such passion.

Latics fan Colin Heaton recalled, *"One fan in the Chaddy End was a big fella and quite scary. He cleared his throat and spat a horrible thing that was so big it was twisting and turning as it flew through the air onto another Oldham fan. He shouted, 'There's there's some Brylcreem for you.' A lot of people laughed as it hit the fan on the back of the head. I nearly threw up but nobody was going argue with this bloke as he was massive. I never saw him again after that and suspect that he was a Hammers fan in the Oldham end waiting for trouble."*

Another fan said, *"I always remember the West Ham League Cup game. I have never seen a game where a manager so tactically outwitted his opponent. Right from the start Marshall went from centre half to play as a second centre forward, leaving Barrett, who was so fast, to cover on his own. West Ham didn't seem to realise what was happening and certainly didn't adjust tactically. Very soon they were three or four down and the* tie was more or less over though there were a few scares in the second leg at Upton Park."

A sponsor of the club reiterated Rick's Black Ladd story, *"As we had sponsored the club we went down on the plane for the replay with the team. We stayed at Waltham Abbey, arriving about 2:00pm. The players went for a sleep while we went out to the local hostelry for a few hours. The team played like they'd been with us and we should have been four down in the first twenty minutes. However, it all worked out somehow. We flew back and went for steak and chips at the Black Ladd pub in Denshaw with all the team. By 2:00am Denis Irwin was legless... and he didn't even drink. The whole team were almost comatosed but amazingly, just 36 hours later, we were playing Leeds United at home with a 12:00 Good Friday kick off. We won 3-1 but God only knows how! We were later told that Joe absolutely slaughtered them in the dressing room at half time. After the meal I got dropped off at home by Rick Holden in his red Ford Cosworth at about 5:00am. It was one of the best days of my life. I could of course tell you about how we actually helped Joe pick the team for that game...."*

Amusing Anecdote 21: On a personal note I watched the game wearing a traditional tall blue and white banded top hat of which two were made by my mate in premature anticipation of the trip to Wembley for the final. After this match we decided to look after them as they would now definitely be needed. Walking back home from Boundary Park was quite an experience as everyone was buoyant with the result. Two of my upper sixth students from the grammar school where I taught, on seeing the top hats, exclaimed in jovial mood to their pals, *"Would you let this man teach your kids?"* I was so euphoric that I had no intention of admonishing them in front of so many other jubilant Oldham fans – it simply added to the excitement of the night which everyone had got caught up in. Perhaps, on that night, the students realised that teachers are not just 'stand up and pontificate' manikins, but that they actually have a real life! Not to show too much of a bias two West Ham fans were walking away from the ground and were overheard to say, *"Well pal, we'll never forget our first trip to Oldham."* The reply was a solemn, *"No!"*

Oldham v Sheffield Wednesday
Second Division – 1990/91 3-2.

Saturday 11th May 1991
Boundary Park 3:00pm

OLDHAM		SHEFFIELD WEDNESDAY
Jon Hallworth	1	Kevin Pressman
Gunnar Halle	2	Roland Nilsson
Andy Barlow	3	Phil King
Nick Henry	4	Carlton Palmer
Earl Barrett	5	Jon Newsome
Richard Jobson	6	Viv Anderson
Neil Adams	7	Danny Wilson
Paul Bernard	8	John Sheridan
Ian Marshall	9	David Hirst
Paul Moulden	10	Gordon Watson
Rick Holden	11	Nigel Worthington
Neil Redfearn	12	Paul Williams
Paul Kane	14	John Harkes
Manager: Joe Royle		Manager: Ron Atkinson

Referee: V Callow (Solihull). Linesmen: JB Robinson (Wigan); E.Hannah (Chester).

Crowd: 18,809

I have saved, in my opinion, the best until last. It is the best because it was the final act of a season which saw Oldham as genuine winners after two years of great, but ultimately heroic failures. It sems a bit harsh to say this because I know that all Latics fans who witnessed the fantastic 'Great Games' (those which I selected are only my opinion) will cherish the wins and events with fondness for as long as they live. But to me, as a professional footballer, I needed the closure on this journey. We had to be champions. Entering this game against promotion achieving Sheffield Wednesday under Ron Atkinson we were in a poor position.

Our vanquished opponents from the League Cup semi-final the year before, West Ham only had to avoid defeat at home to play-off chasing Notts County. Wednesday were a tough team and we had had a great game against them earlier in the season at Hillsborough, when they fought back with two penalties to claim a 2-2 draw in front of a massive 35,000 crowd. We were under no illusions as to the difficulty of the task ahead.

We started nervously and soon conceded a goal when David Hirst headed in a rebound off the crossbar which went in off the post! We pushed for an equalizer but, given the chance, I shot woefully wide when I should have scored. Just before half time we should have been 2-0 down when Hirst again headed onto the post only this time it stayed out.

During the interval I was pacing up and down nervously and couldn't wait to get back out there. It then began to get worse as we fell to a superb half-volley from Danny Wilson from outside the box. I can remember thinking that we had blown it and it was going to be West Ham's day. To make matters worse, news had filtered through that the Hammers were losing 2-0 to Neil Warnock's County and that would have really rubbed salt into the wound! Then I literally did rub slt into the wound making my only real contribution of the match. Our first goal came out of me running back towards the half way line and making a slide tackle on a Wednesday player from the side. In doing this it tore a huge scab off my hip and I can remember, like it happened yesterday, the agony of it. If you look the incident up on *YouTube* you will see me roll over in obvious pain for an instant before sitting up and watching as the pain subsided. The ball worked via Andy Barlow's cross, who had a tremendous game, to Marshy, who prodded home his second attempt with the outside of his foot. The commentator said that the goal came from 'absolutely nowhere!' It fu**in' didn't, it came from skill and determination.

We then put the pressure on but couldn't force an equalizer and suddenly we were in danger of conceding a goal on the break as that was all that Wednesday had left. Jon Hallworth had had a brilliant season in goals for us and made the best save, in terms of importance, of his career when he dived at the feet of John Sheridan to prevent us from losing the championship and ruining the whole season. Things were getting desperate now. Then came a huge slice of luck; after a good cross from Neil Redfearn, Paul Bernard hit a first time half-volley (half-volley again) which took a deflection and flew in the bottom corner.

The drama and tension was unreal. The fans spilled onto the pitch as if we had won it, such was the fever in the ground. Time was running out and if it stayed like that we would be the bridesmaids. We then turned on intense pressure and a shot was closed down from Paul Moulden who then retrieved it and tried a cross. The ball bounced loose in the area and on came Andy Barlow to nick it ahead of Sheridan. He was clipped and went down. More ecstatic fan involvement as they roared onto the pitch. Penalty! All the two years of drama in our footballing lives for those involved in the epic cup games had culminated in a cup-tie type finish to an entire league season. You couldn't have written it like this and indeed you wouldn't want to, just for the state of your nerves.

The referee delayed the taking of the penalty as he booked Sheridan but Redders was the coolest man in the ground and I just knew we could rely on him. He hammered it past Pressman's right hand and into the bottom corner. Then it was chaos. The pitch invasion was the best I had ever witnessed and it helped to calm us down as the stewards tried to get everyone off the pitch for Wednesday to take the kick-off. As soon as they did, the referee blew for full-time and guess what? Another pitch invasion! We ran like hell for the dressing room! In the sanctuary of the dressing room there were tears of joy to be winners at last. What a buzz – one of the greatest feelings of my life and I am sure that the lads and management felt the same. Champagne was sprayed everywhere and it went all over my gear. I didn't care!

Once again you had to feel for West Ham. They were about to receive the trophy when they got the stunning news that we had won the title and the trophy had to be flown up by helicopter to Boundary Park. Earl Barrett, as captain, was presented with some plastic trophy from the club shop but we didn't care, again, as it was just a symbol. The thing that mattered was that finally, after all this time, we had won a major trophy and could be called champions of the division we had set our sights on winning, and getting out of two years earlier.

That night we all went out in Oldham and joined the fans in celebration. They played a massive part and the town was packed to the rafters. They never stopped believing and it spurred us on to achieve. The next day's open top bus ride with the real trophy meant something and the fans turned out in their thousands to celebrate. And, unlike the one from 1990s League Cup Final, I was standing up at the front with the other lads waving to the crowd instead of being pissed up on the back of the top seat lying on my back. That was, in my opinion, our greatest game of that era but it may not have been so for all. It certainly was the one where all the drama exploded and put a seal on our time on the plastic paradise.

The manager had put his side together for less than £1m, and he did it quite cannily by reversing the conventional big club – small club relationship. He had somehow picked the pockets of Everton, Leeds and Manchester City of gems that they didn't even know they owned. Things were happening that didn't usually happen at 'unfashionable' clubs. *Shoot* magazine did a

photo-shoot with the team and local band the *Inspiral Carpets;*
even Rick Holden was in demand as he appeared on the TV
show *A Question of Sport.* 'Big Joe' had even received a letter of
congratulations from 10 Downing Street. Oldham Athletic were
officially established as everybody's favourite second team!

Team spirit was at the highest and they never knew when they
were beaten; they always followed a lost cause and never gave
in. Team bonding had reached a new high off the field. In an age
when footballers did not have to conform to special diets and
individual training their camaraderie was often bonded by
having a good time and drinking alcohol – no wonder they were
successful, they were having fun! Success breeds more success.
They never took themselves too seriously; Holden and Andy
Rhodes even hammed it up for an Alas Smith and Jones skit.

After ex-manager Jimmy Frizzell had described Mike Milligan
as a yard dog, because of his terrier like approach to the
midfield role, the club sold 3,000 inflatable yard dogs – these
were the days of inflatables which originated with a five foot
banana. I even witnessed a supporter inside Boundary Park with
a blown up dingy with oars – the mind boggles! Everything was
fun. It was noted that Nick Henry wasn't scoring as many goals
as Mike Milligan so he was instructed 'tongue-in-cheek' by Joe
that if he got a chance to shoot, he should pass it! The feelgood
fantasy of the Latics made the whole country smile. It is
important to note that before the 1989/90 season Oldham had
not beaten a top-flight side for 66 years; then it all happened and
Royle's barmy army didn't just beat their superiors, they
absolutely annihilated them and they did it by playing a high-
class brand of football.

Back to the job in hand.... Joe's pre-match round-up stated,
*"Welcome back to Boundary Park for our penultimate game on
our plastic pitch, which has been the subject of such controversy
since it was laid five years ago. In the first year of its existence
we made the play-offs only to be cruelly denied a chance of
Division One by the away goals ruling, so it's maybe a case of
poetic justice that we should attain promotion in the final
season of the pitches existence. I hope that as I write these notes
the Owls have already been promoted after their Wednesday*

fixture against Bristol City (which they were), there are certainly going to be so many permutations." Joe was spot on and everybody wanted to witness the outcome.

The match was a sell out and if it could match the excitement from the earlier 2-2 encounter at Hillsborough, which attracted the biggest Second Division crowd of the season at 34,845), it would be some match. Wednesday were allocated 3,000 tickets and the Rochdale Road end was fenced off to accommodate a further 2,000 home fans. No-one could have ever predicted what was to occur in the ensuing 90 minutes of football.

In one of the most remarkable and memorable games ever staged at Boundary Park, Sheffield Wednesday came to spoil the party for championship seeking Athletic. It was the last day of the season and West Ham United were in top spot, Athletic were second and Wednesday occupied third spot. To make it even more interesting the Hammers were entertaining fourth placed Notts County. West Ham lost 2-1 at home to County but as news filtered through to Upton Park that Athletic were losing 2-0 at home the Boleyn celebrations began. Athletic remarkably pulled back the score to 2-2 in regulation time but even a draw was enough to give the Hammers the trophy. With all other games ended, the referee, Vic Callow, allowed some extra time to compensate for the time wasting antics of Wednesday.

After 92 minutes of pulsating football, John Sheridan brought down Andy Barlow for a penalty to the home side. It was 'Roy of the Rovers' stuff now! The penalty became the last kick of the last game on the last day of the season. Not even Hans Christian Anderson could have written the script. Neil Redfearn, cool as a cucumber, stepped up to take the kick but then the referee stopped the kick to book a Sheffield player. It all added to the tension. When Redders dispatched his 90th minute penalty – there was no 90 + 7 minutes in those days – the whole of Boundary Park, except for the Wednesday contingent, went into a frenzy of excited celebration with raptures of unashamed emotion and tears of joy. It was his most important goal ever and many of the Oldham fans had covered their eyes as they couldn't even watch it. Fans invaded the pitch to celebrate and in true World Cup type commentary they thought it was all over

– well, it was now! Athletic were back in the big time. They had done it! No longer the 'bridesmaids' as Oldham Athletic had tied the knot and were now married to the First Division after a gap of 68 years! The impossible dream had become reality. It was the pinnacle of supporting Oldham Athletic.

The open-top celebration with the trophy

Amusing Anecdote 22: With all the confusion of this match, and with the Hammers prematurely celebrating their 'championship win' the championship trophy had already been delivered to Upton Park as West Ham were odds-on favourites to win it. Only something astonishingly unexpected could have changed the outcome, but change it did – such was Oldham Athletic! The championship trophy had to be hurridely redirected to Boundary Park, only to arrived by courier with West Ham's name engraved on it – much to the embarrassment of League officials! The club shop immediately rectified the mistake.

Oldham fan Fryatt quoted, *"I never believed in fate until this game but it is difficult to find words that fit this encounter as it was unreal. The Owls took the lead early on in the first half and then it all kicked-off in the Chaddy End. The result was that about 30 Wednesday fans were booted out of the ground and the game was consequently held up for seven minutes. It was to play a massive part of what went on in the aftermath. Oldham went two down and it looked all over but that man again, Ian Marshall, pulled one back four minutes from time. My immediate thought was 'consolation.' However, the Oldham machine did it again and Paul Bernard equalised just before time was up. It was still on! It went into injury time; remember I mentioned fate and that seven minutes? As the seven minutes were concluded, and with the referee's whistle at his lips to blow for time, John Sheridan lunged at the ball in the penalty box and down went Andy Barlow, which he later described as, "I went down like a sack of spuds!" Time seemed to stand still. The referee pointed to the spot. Neil Redfearn did not flinch – get in! Back in the town after the game Yorkshire Street was closed to traffic from 6:00pm. Such was the joy that evening that I think I eventually woke up on Monday."*

Another supporter said, *"I told my missus, if we win and West Ham lose, don't expect me home at a reasonable hour and in a reasonable state. Plenty of the opposing fans in the Chaddy at the start before they got shifted to the Rochdale Road End. There was a full range of emotions throughout the game and I was on the pitch at the end. There's a picture of me somewhere on the roof of the Latics' dugout. I was also one of the group of people that were carrying Rick Holden head high! After the game we went to the Spinners Arms on Chadderton Way and there were eight Wednesday fans in, so I bought them all a whisky whether they wanted it or not. Up town after, Yorkshire Street was closed to traffic because of the celebrations. Happy days! I don't remember going home. Let's hope it can happen again one day for the young uns going now."*

Colin Heaton remarked, *"I was in the Chaddy End when they scored their first goal and the Wednesday fans started to jump up and down. Me and a few of my friends got caught up in the fracas and I was punched in the face, but I have to say it was from a lightweight and I didn't flinch. I was horrified and chased them down to the front thinking I could take on the world. Lots of yard dogs were throwing punches a plenty."*

A euphoric Latics' fan recalled, *"The Sheffield Wednesday game will never be beaten. It was fairy tale stuff. My seat was in the*

Main Stand and was right next to the directors box. I swear that when Redfearn scored the penalty, I was the only one looking at the pitch. They ware great memories."

After the match Joe Royle declared, *"It was tremendous – what a way for the season to end. But we've played to the end all season. The players never know when they're beaten, so perhaps it was fitting. We were 10 minutes away from finishing in third place, and suddenly we were champions with virtually the last kick of the season."*

Everton manager Howard Kendall said of Joe, *"Joe's done a tremendous job for Oldham, and it's great that they will be in the Frist Division next season. His side play imaginative and attractive football, and he's brought them a long way from those early days. He's made as big a success of his career as a manager as he did when he was a player and I'm pleased for him."*

At the civic reception Mayor Sid Jacobs announced, *"You're a credit to Oldham. You have brought a lot of prestige to the town and the people of Oldham, and the council are very grateful indeed."*

Councillor John Battye added, *"We are very proud of the way things have gone, not only for the club, but for the town. A lot of people are backing Oldham, not just from Oldham but from the rest of the country. There's been no sour taste in the mouths of people that other teams have left behind. This is not the end – this is just the start. After yesterday, we can believe anything."*

The players had their say too. Earl Barratt: *"Hopefully, this is the sign of things to come."* Andy Barlow: *"We've done this for Oldham."* Andy Ritchie: *"It's been a fantastic season – we can't believe it. It will be nice to get back in the First Division. I'm looking forwards to playing against the best defences again – the Liverpools and the Arsenals. The crowds up here will love it – they've been starved of seeing these teams for so long."* Richard Jobson: *"I didn't realise there were so many people in Oldham. Here's to the First Division."* Rick Holden: *"The last few year's we've done something, but in the last 10 years Roger*

Palmer's got you lot promoted. You'd better turn up tomorrow night (for his testimonial), or you aren't worth a sod!" And the fans certainly listened as 17,500 of them turned up for the match against Manchester City, which the Latics won 3-2. Of course 'Oooohh Roger Palmer' bowed out, as expected, with the second goal of the competitively fought game – how fitting.

What it's all about - a championship medal at last

Oldham v Southampton
Premier League – 1992/93 4-3.

Saturday 8th May 1993
Boundary Park 3:00pm

OLDHAM		SOUTHAMPTON
Paul Gerrard	1	Tim Flowers
Richard Jobson	2	Jeff Kenna
Steve Redmond	3	Ken Monkou
Neil Pointon	4	Micky Adams
Craig Fleming	5	Nicky Banger
Nick Henry	6	Glenn Cockerill
Gunnar Halle	7	Tommy Widdrington
Mike Milligan	8	Neil Maddison
Andy Ritchie	9	Matt Le Tissier
Ian Olney	10	Iain Dowie
Paul Bernard	11	Richard Hall
Ian Marshall	12	Kevin Moore
John Keeley	14	Francis Benali
Neil Adams	15	Ian Andrews
Manager: Joe Royle		Manager: Ian Branfoot

Referee: H King (Merthyr Tydfil)

Crowd: 14,597

Bonus Review from Andy Ritchie ......

We had our remit – win and hope that Arsenal beat Crystal Palace at Highbury. We were great at home and Southampton had a miserable away record, only 3 wins. Joe gave us the rally cry as we went out onto the Boundary Park pitch, *"Don't leave anything in the dressing room, if you're knackered we can sub you."* We'd given ourselves a chance to survive the 'drop' by winning our last two games of the three that we had to win to stand a chance. I had had a nightmare with injuries and was only starting my 10th game, but was eager to play my part in the 'great escape.' The 'R' word had not been mentioned at all, Joe and Willie had banned it; we had beat Aston Villa away and Liverpool at home to set up this final day nerve jangler.

I and all the lads had faith in our ability to get the job finished, the hard work was already, done wasn't it? We were all pumped! Running out onto the pitch only enhanced my determination. The Oldham faithful went bonkers when I arrived for the warm up. I recall the start of the game was a frantic pace and I put Gunnar Halle through early on, only for Southampton to scramble his effort clear. Both teams had chances early on and Le Tissier also had a shot cleared off the line like Halle's. Southampton had assured survival two weeks earlier and had therefore, nothing to play for other than professional pride and the honour to the other clubs threatened with the 'R' word. They were certainly doing that, fuelled by something other than pride. We had heard a rumour that the Saints had been out the night before and that their tanks were full and so they were trying extra hard to win!! The initial trading of blows at high tension ensued but we coped. Adrenalin is a wonderful thing.

Our first goal came in an unusual fashion with a more unusual scorer, 'Nino' Pointon, our left back. It went direct from a corner from our right into the left station; he swung it in with pace and swerve, avoiding everyone, aided by the wind which as always was blowing in our favour towards the Chaddy End in the first half. 1-0 on 29 minutes and it was a relief to hit the opening blow. I felt happy with my game and was heavily involved with play. Five minutes later I lost the ball to their captain, Glenn Cockerill, and in trying to regain possession I fouled him. They punted the free-kick to Dowie who managed to find Le Tissier via Maddison and he volleyed home from 15 yards so it was 1-1 in the 34th minute.

Near the end of the half Nino went close again it was becoming a great game as he volleyed over. Our second goal came from a long free-kick. I flicked the ball on and it ended up with Gunnar capitalizing on it by arriving late to stab the ball to Inspector Gadget (Ian Olney) to prod it home. It was 2-1 on 44 minutes and we had noses in front again. Flem (Craig Fleming) missed a great chance to send us 3-1 up at the break but we were now on top and running that extra mile for each other.

The referee blew for the interval and I remember not wanting to go in at half time as it could stop our momentum. Not to have held on to the lead longer, and to have gifted them a goal, we gained belief and rallied round in the dressing room at half time and I had a feeling that we could win! Joe and all the staff had to try to get their points across in a way that it sank in, whilst not destroying our hyper state, so as to not to take it out of us in the next 45 minutes, the biggest 45 minutes of our careers.

We started quickly and Reddo (Steve Redmond) had a shot which just whistled wide after a surging run. We kept the pressure up with more marauding runs from Craig Fleming and Gunnar, with whom I seemed to have had a telepathic relationship with on this day. It culminated with his cross to the near post which I buried with my head, 3-1 on 55 minutes. This was both elation and pleasure, and what I was in the team to do. On 65 minutes Terry (Nick Henry) slipped the ball to me just inside their half. I went off on the half turn and knew that I was free and again I saw my man Gunnar, and slid the ball into his path. He was one-on-one with Flowers and, despite him getting a hand to the ball, Gunnar made it 4-1 in the 65th minute. We were home and dry, weren't we?

I was replaced in the 70th minute by Ogrond (Ian Marshall) and so had to watch and kick the last 20 minutes from the bench. I remember feeling so helpless and frustrated not to be out there, but I was gone due to the lack of games. My bolt was truly shot and it was time for fresh legs and Marshy had plenty of them! I remember the time passing so slowly sitting there and watched Marshy and Gunnar waste two great chances; sitters, I would say. In between this time Le Tissier had done his usual in scoring a 25 yard free-kick, the classic one which bounced up and over our keeper Paul Gerrard. I thought the pitch was conspiring against us as it was 4-2 on 67 minutes. This was becoming agony and we shot ourselves in the foot when we allowed Le Tissier to score an uncharacteristic header to make it 4-3 on 85 minutes.

Everybody in the ground, including Joe with a radio in his pocket, knew that Palace were 3-0 down at Arsenal and the anxiety was fever pitch. Joe went to the top of the tunnel and joined in the screaming at the referee who had found so much injury time which is still a mystery to all to this day. He had his parentage questioned and Joe was going crackers at him. At last the final whistle, I remember looking at Joe standing there with his arms aloft, being hugged by all and sundry and me and Bert (Neil Adams) with our arms around each other rejoicing.

The pitch was mobbed and so were we, the players. We had done it. *The Great Escape!* Whereas Steve McQueen had slid into the barbed wire fence when trying to free himself, we had managed to jump over it on our motorbike of grit and determination – team spirit. The feeling was amazing and, of course, the celebrations went on for a long time, days and weeks! It was a pleasure and an honour to have been involved that day and playing a part in our survival, and to have been associated with such a marvellous bunch of talented professionals and dear friends (nutters mainly) whilst playing for Oldham Athletic.

Thanks to all the players, staff and the board of directors; and especially to the fans who cheered us along every inch of the way. This was a another chapter of the 'Pinch me Years!'

Andy Ritchie

Rick's Review (as a fan) ......

This was a truly great game of the golden era, but one I didn't feature in because of my move to Manchester City. I did however, witness it as a fan from a distance and I will give you my take on it as it was unique.

I had been a fan of Leeds United as a child and hated the miscarriages of justice which always seemed to befall them. Growing up in Yorkshire, it was only natural to support Leeds United as they were one of the top sides in England and Europe. I experienced elation when Leeds won the FA Cup 1972 and the League and several UEFA Cups. I also experienced the gut wrenching feelings of disappointment when we failed to beat Sunderland in the 1973 FA Cup Final and the disgrace of the injustice of the game in the European Cup Final against Bayern Munich in 1975.

I continued to support Leeds but as I got older and became a player I became a bit more neutral and focussed more on my professional role as a job rather than being a fan. I had started to become hardened to the professional game. Of course I looked out for Leeds' results and those of Burnley, Halifax and Watford, for whom I had previously played. You never lose your ties and interest in clubs you have been involved in! Today I add Oldham, Manchester City, Blackpool and Barnsley to my list. However, in 1993, on the last day of the season I once again became a true football fan. This was the incredible great escape acts of all time with Oldham getting results against Liverpool, Manchester United, Aston Villa and finally in the last game of the season against Southampton. This was a game that the Latics had to win and they took everyone down to the wire as usual.

I was playing for City at Maine Road in a meaningless game, points wise, for us. The truth was that I couldn't fully concentrate and focus on what I was doing on the pitch as I was concerned for Oldham Athletic, the club, and of course the management, the players who were my mates and of course the fans, many of whom I did count as friends and knew very well. It was a tense and fraught day for all at Boundary Park and the whole nation tuned into this fascinating scenario.

I kept hearing the reports of the scoring at Boundary Park coming through via radio from fans in the crowd. The City fans were shouting out the score to me from the Kippax Stand as they knew I was more than interested in the score. I wasn't nervous or anxious, just concerned that they might get some outrageous bad luck and all the hard work would have been in vain. It was tough following it from afar so God only knows what it was like watching it unfold in front of you! I could really empathise.

Our game finished before the Oldham game and it resulted in a 5-2 loss. I shot off the pitch as a quick as I could before our end of season lap of dishonour to our fans. I listened to the last few agonising moments on the radio, which Tony Book had sorted in the dressing room. It seemed to just consist of Southampton bombarding Oldham. Finally it was over and I swear you could hear the roars live from just a few miles up the road, and I could breathe a sigh of relief. It was tense and I didn't want to be a fan of this type of stuff – it could be bad for your health!

I later rang the club and spoke to Willie Donachie and then rushed through to Oldham to meet the lads. Needless to say, it was some night and I was treated like one of the Oldham players by the fans. They forgave my move to City, for that night at least. So I can say, with genuine experience, that I empathise will the fans and all their range of emotions and senses and feel sorry for the stuff we put you through during these 14 Great Games. Enjoy the re-run.

Rick

Dave - "'Ave we finished now Rick?"

Rick - "Yes we have – thank God for that – writing about it after all these years has knackered me more than when I was playing! Come On Oldham!"